Alliances and the Developing World

Allan Grieve
(Assistant Head Teacher Falkirk High School)

Graeme Pont
(Principal Teacher of Modern Studies Cults Academy)

Pulse Publications

CONTENTS

TO THE TEACHER

Chapter 4 of this book is not required for Standard Grade Modern Studies. It is intended to support Intermediate 1 and 2 Modern Studies. However, students following a Standard Grade course may also find the material useful as the skills used in the source-based questions are identical to those required for Standard Grade.

ACKNOWLEDGEMENTS

The authors and publishers would like to thank the following for permission to reproduce copyright material: The Press Association for photographs on pages 4, 5, 6, 11, 12, 14, 15, 20, 21, 22, 29, 31, 37, 52, 53, 54, 59, 68, 70, 71, 76. UN photo library for photos on pages 25, 26, 27, 28, 65, 67. NATO for photos on pages 51, 56, 58, 59, 60, 64.

Published and typeset by
Pulse Publications
45 Raith Road, Fenwick,
Ayrshire, KA3 6DB

Printed and bound by
Thomson Colour Printers

British Library Cataloguing-in-Publication Data
A Catalogue record for this book is available from the British Library
ISBN 0 948 766 88 3
© Grieve & Pont 2003

THE POLITICS OF AID
WHY DO SOME AFRICAN COUNTRIES NEED AID?

DEVELOPED COUNTRIES

Industrialised countries such as the United Kingdom, Japan, the USA, France, Germany, the Netherlands and Canada are often referred to as developed countries. Typically, such countries share similar social and economic circumstances such as a high standard of living, a good health service, high levels of literacy, low rates of infant mortality and economies based on industry, commerce, insurance and new technology.

Such countries are also referred to as the Rich North. As a consequence of being rich, with advanced industries, such countries have considerable power. They can affect what happens to the lives of people in many parts of the world—especially in developing continents such as Africa.

DEVELOPING COUNTRIES

These countries are concentrated in the southern hemisphere. Most African countries, India, South American countries and many Asian nations make up this group. Countries which can be categorised as developing share similar social and economic problems. Their needs are similar. For example, developing countries would share the following: a low standard of living, low levels of health care, high levels of illiteracy, high infant mortality rates and economies which are based on agriculture, a limited range of exports and labour-intensive, poorly skilled means of production. Many of these countries require aid or assistance from developed countries which means that the country giving the aid can have power or influence over the country which receives it.

Such nations are also referred to as the Third World or the Poor South.

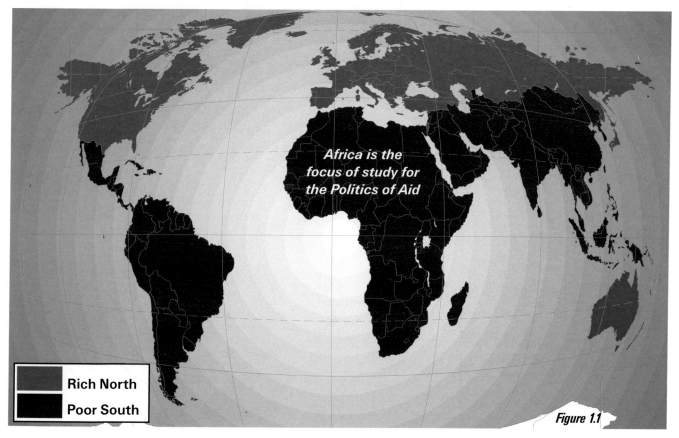

Africa is the focus of study for the Politics of Aid

Rich North
Poor South

Figure 1.1

INFANT MORTALITY RATES

The infant mortality rate is perhaps the best indicator that we have of the needs of a country. If a child's needs are being met well in the first year of life, it is highly likely that there will be a low infant mortality rate.

If a country does not have many of the seven factors shown in Figure 1.2, then the children of that country have a greater chance of failing to reach their first birthday. The less that is done to assist such countries, the greater the problem will become. For a country to meet its needs it must develop its ability to create wealth to pay for, and continue to operate, the services it requires.

Often only a simple action is needed to break into a cycle of poverty or deprivation, leading to a whole series of problems being solved. Figure 1.3 illustrates how one problem can lead to another. However, the cycle can be broken into at a variety of points, thereby changing a cycle of deprivation into a cycle of success.

ACTIVITIES

1. What are the differences between developed and developing countries?
2. Explain why any four factors in Figure 1.2 could result in lower infant mortality rates.
3. Study Figure 1.3. Explain how one problem in the cycle can lead to a series of other problems.
4. Choose one point in the cycle and explain how help or aid at this point could break the cycle.
5. Draw a 'Cycle of Wealth', showing how aid would lead to a change at each stage, resulting in wealth rather than poverty.

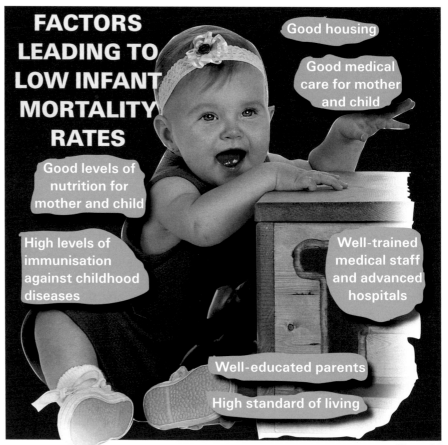

Figure 1.2

Figure 1.3

WHY DO SOME AFRICAN COUNTRIES NEED AID?

Many countries in Africa face a range of social, economic and political problems that hamper development and make economic and social progress difficult. No one factor explains why these countries face the challenges that they do. Large numbers of African people have needs that are not being met. To achieve an understanding of the most pressing needs many African people face, we will focus on a number of country profiles and consider a range of statistical data and issues.

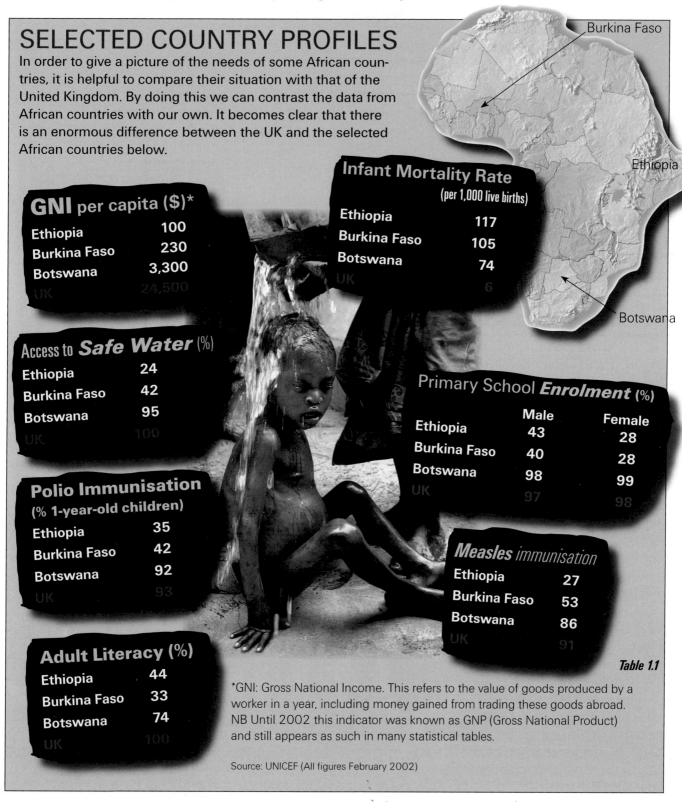

SELECTED COUNTRY PROFILES

In order to give a picture of the needs of some African countries, it is helpful to compare their situation with that of the United Kingdom. By doing this we can contrast the data from African countries with our own. It becomes clear that there is an enormous difference between the UK and the selected African countries below.

Burkina Faso

Ethiopia

Botswana

GNI per capita ($)*

Ethiopia	100
Burkina Faso	230
Botswana	3,300
UK	24,500

Infant Mortality Rate
(per 1,000 live births)

Ethiopia	117
Burkina Faso	105
Botswana	74
UK	6

Access to Safe Water (%)

Ethiopia	24
Burkina Faso	42
Botswana	95
UK	100

Primary School Enrolment (%)

	Male	Female
Ethiopia	43	28
Burkina Faso	40	28
Botswana	98	99
UK	97	98

Polio Immunisation
(% 1-year-old children)

Ethiopia	35
Burkina Faso	42
Botswana	92
UK	93

Measles immunisation

Ethiopia	27
Burkina Faso	53
Botswana	86
UK	91

Adult Literacy (%)

Ethiopia	44
Burkina Faso	33
Botswana	74
UK	100

Table 1.1

*GNI: Gross National Income. This refers to the value of goods produced by a worker in a year, including money gained from trading these goods abroad. NB Until 2002 this indicator was known as GNP (Gross National Product) and still appears as such in many statistical tables.

Source: UNICEF (All figures February 2002)

1 If you compare the African countries in the profiles with the UK, what conclusions do you come to?

2 Of the three African countries in the profiles, which is most in need of aid? Give detailed reasons for your answer.

3 What do you consider to be the three greatest needs which are shared by the African countries in the profiles? Give detailed reasons to support your view.

4 "Infant mortality rates are good indicators of the needs of a country." Explain why this might be the case.

ISSUE: HIV/AIDS

There is an AIDS epidemic in Africa. Africa is home to 70% of the adults and 80% of the children in the world living with HIV. The scale of the problem is huge, with 12.1 million children having been orphaned up to 1997. In 1999 alone there were 2,204,200 AIDS-related deaths. It is estimated that over 28.1 million Africans were living with HIV/AIDS by the end of 2001. Currently there is no known cure for the illness, which is ultimately fatal.

AIDS is more deadly than the effects of war. In 1998, 200,000 Africans died in wars, while more than 2 million died of AIDS. Evidence shows that as HIV/AIDS rates increase in a country, there is a significant fall in GDP*. In African countries with 20% or more of the population infected, GDP may decline by up to 2% a year. Key workers and professional who are necessary for development, such as farmers, agricultural workers

FACTFILE: Aids Orphans

Of the 13.2 million AIDS orphans in the world, 95% live in Africa.

Most people who contract AIDS become infected before they are 25 and die by the time they turn 35, leaving behind a generation of children to be raised by grandparents or left on their own.

AIDS orphans are very vulnerable in countries where communities can barely fend for themselves, let alone cater for the needs of these children.

Such children are often at greater risk of illness, abuse, sexual exploitation and malnutrition. Their growth is often stunted and most do not receive health care.

Older children often take on the role of a mother or father to their younger brothers or sisters. They live in extreme poverty without services or support.

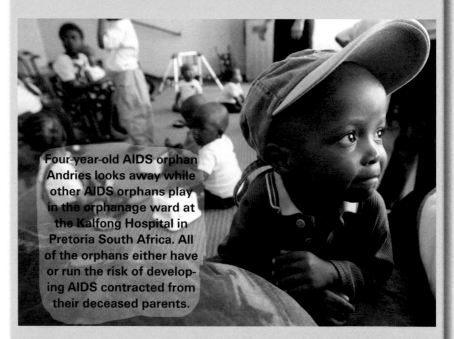

Four-year-old AIDS orphan Andries looks away while other AIDS orphans play in the orphanage ward at the Kalfong Hospital in Pretoria South Africa. All of the orphans either have or run the risk of developing AIDS contracted from their deceased parents.

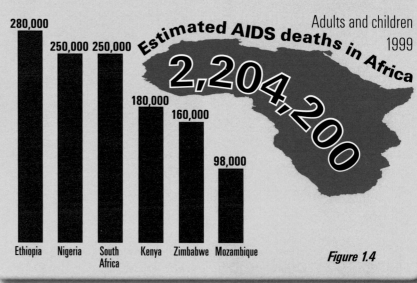

Estimated AIDS deaths in Africa

Adults and children 1999

2,204,200

Ethiopia	Nigeria	South Africa	Kenya	Zimbabwe	Mozambique
280,000	250,000	250,000	180,000	160,000	98,000

Figure 1.4

and teachers, are falling victim to AIDS. The East African Standard reported on 2 July 2001 that economic growth in Africa had fallen by as much as 4% due to AIDS.

*GDP—Gross Domestic Product. Unlike GNI, GDP does not take into account the value of goods accounted for in foreign trade. GDP is the annual value of goods and services provided in a country.

In an attempt to meet the needs faced by their people, many African countries have borrowed money from the World Bank or the International Monetary Fund (IMF). However, interest has to be paid back on a loan, a situation which has lead to extreme hardship for a number of countries. Crop failures, wars, a drop in the market price of the main export of the country, drought, floods and a range of other disasters have left countries such as Sudan with a massive debt to repay. If money has to be spent on repaying debts, this often results in cuts in essential social services such as health and education. In a number of African countries the debt to be paid back in a year is greater than the GNI of the country.

There is a continuing campaign to cancel debt in developing countries. The Jubilee Coalition in 2000 mounted a powerful campaign to get world governments to end the debt crisis. The leaflet above is from the campaign.

The cost of debt

Innocent people are paying for the debt burden with their lives. In order to meet debt repayments, the governments of poor countries are having to penalise the poor by cutting back on expenditure and making them pay for essential services.

In Tanzania the government has had to introduce fees for schooling, drugs and medical treatment.

"The debt burden is killing people because they cannot afford to go to hospital. If they don't have drugs they die. This is a direct result of the debt crisis."
Canon HP Mtingele, General Secretary of the Church of the Province of Tanzania

Is there a solution?

Yes. The leaders of the world's richest governments have the power to end the debt crisis. They now control most of the debts either directly or through the big financial institutions. They can easily afford to cancel the necessary amounts. But they are simply not doing enough.

Christian Aid/Elaine Duigenan

Esther Ngairo (left) of Milo village, Tanzania, is not sure her new-born baby Joyce will survive. If Joyce gets ill, Esther will not have the money to pay for treatment.

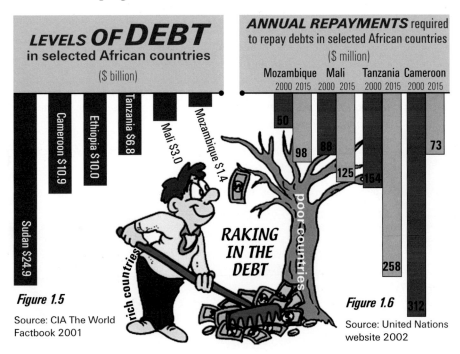

LEVELS OF DEBT
in selected African countries
($ billion)

Sudan $24.9
Cameroon $10.9
Ethiopia $10.0
Tanzania $6.8
Mali $3.0
Mozambique $1.4

rich countries
poor countries

RAKING IN THE DEBT

Figure 1.5

Source: CIA The World Factbook 2001

ANNUAL REPAYMENTS required to repay debts in selected African countries
($ million)

	Mozambique		Mali		Tanzania		Cameroon	
	2000	2015	2000	2015	2000	2015	2000	2015
	50	98	88	125	154	258	73	312

Figure 1.6

Source: United Nations website 2002

THE POLITICS OF AID
WHY CAN SOME COUNTRIES NOT MEET THEIR NEEDS?

What you will learn

1 The social, economic and political reasons which explain why some African countries experience famine.

2 The reasons why Sudan has experienced famine.

Ray Bush, a lecturer in Politics at the University of Leeds, has written an article entitled Explaining Africa's Famine. He challenges the view that it is factors such as climate, drought or crop failure which cause famine (an extreme shortage of food). After all, such climatic factors affect other developing countries, but they do not suffer famine to the extent that the Sudan, Somalia or Ethiopia have over the last ten years.

As a social scientist, Ray Bush looks for social, economic and political factors to explain fam-

ine. He argues that famine is not caused by 'natural' factors but by 'unnatural' factors created by humankind. In a sentence, he summarises the problem as he sees it: "Famine occurs when the strains on social systems overwhelm the available resources for coping with drought or whatever happens to be the prevailing crisis." Simply stated, this means that when a crisis happens, a country cannot respond to solve that crisis because of social, economic and political factors.

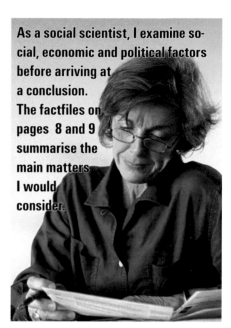

As a social scientist, I examine social, economic and political factors before arriving at a conclusion. The factfiles on pages 8 and 9 summarise the main matters I would consider.

FACTFILE: Social Factors

Question:
What social factors would you look at to explain why a country is suffering from food shortages or famine?

I would consider the following:

The levels of education in a country. Are literacy rates high or low?

The customs and habits of a country. Are farming methods adequate? Does the way in which people live lead to certain problems? Are there traditions which prevent development taking place? Are traditional crops the best ones to grow?

Has there been a drift away from the countryside to the towns, causing unemployment and placing heavy demands on housing, health and other services?

Are wealth and land concentrated in the hands of a few rich families or merchants?

Are there major health and medical issues which lead to ill health, early death and an inability to work efficiently?

What is the attitude towards women? Is the progress of women limited by customs and beliefs?

FACTFILE: Political Factors

Question: What political factors would you look at to explain why a country is suffering from food shortages or famine?

I would consider the following:

Is there war in a country which is causing problems for the economy, e.g. land cannot be farmed because of fighting, movement is not possible?

Is the government in control of the country? Are warring groups stopping aid coming through? Is it safe to transport goods?

Is a government corrupt? Does it spend aid or money from taxes on the military and police while people starve? Does the government spend money foolishly on great projects like airports which benefit a rich few, while the poor majority starve?

Does a government persecute groups within its country and abuse their civil rights? For example, are some groups or tribes given better treatment than others?

Does a government have a communist ideology? If so, does this mean that capitalist nations of the developed world are reluctant to help it?

Has the government supported enemies of major developed nations like the USA or the UK? If so, this may mean that aid will not be given by developed nations.

FACTFILE: Economic Factors

Question: What economic factors would you look at to explain why a country is suffering from food shortages or famine?

I would consider the following:

Is a country in debt to the World Bank or another country? Is that country spending more to repay a loan than it is earning from exports?

What are the levels of Gross Domestic Product (GDP – the annual value of goods produced and services provided in a country) and Gross National Income (GNI – see page 5) in a particular country?

How poor are the people? What levels of wages are paid? How high are levels of unemployment?

What products or raw materials does a country export to generate income? Does it rely on one product or crop where prices can rise and fall leading to financial problems? Is the quality of the product for export of a suitable standard?

Do multi-national companies control the main industries with profits flowing out of the country back to the developed world? Are the workers of such countries being exploited by the multi-national companies which may be paying very low wages or prices for products?

Is the aid being given to the country 'Tied Aid'? In other words, does the country receiving aid have to give something in return?

ACTIVITIES

1 Study the Social Factfile and explain how any four social factors can lead to food shortages.

2 Study the Political Factfile and explain how any four political factors could lead to food shortages.

3 Study the Economic Factfile and describe how any four economic factors can lead to food shortages.

4 Which economic factor do you think is the most important? Give reasons for your answer.

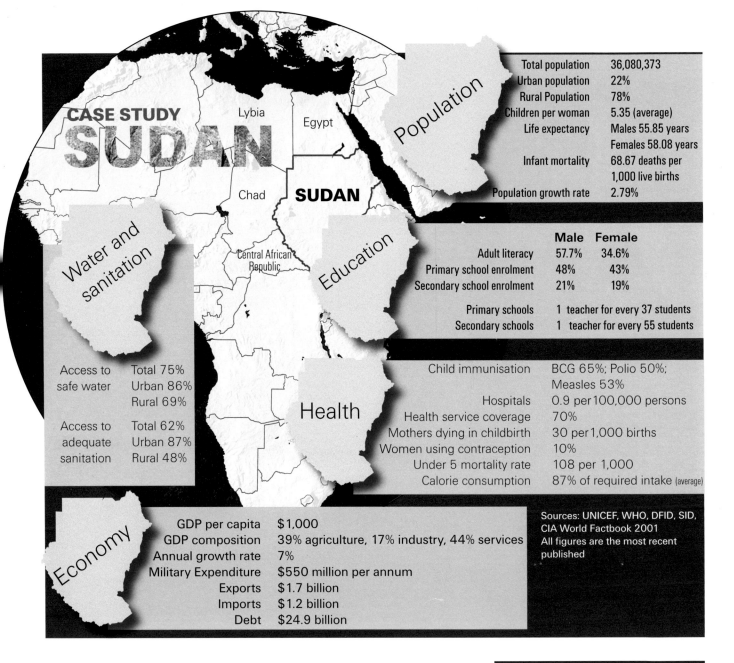

CASE STUDY SUDAN

Population

Total population	36,080,373
Urban population	22%
Rural Population	78%
Children per woman	5.35 (average)
Life expectancy	Males 55.85 years
	Females 58.08 years
Infant mortality	68.67 deaths per
	1,000 live births
Population growth rate	2.79%

Education

	Male	Female
Adult literacy	57.7%	34.6%
Primary school enrolment	48%	43%
Secondary school enrolment	21%	19%

Primary schools	1 teacher for every 37 students
Secondary schools	1 teacher for every 55 students

Water and sanitation

Access to safe water	Total 75%
	Urban 86%
	Rural 69%
Access to adequate sanitation	Total 62%
	Urban 87%
	Rural 48%

Health

Child immunisation	BCG 65%; Polio 50%; Measles 53%
Hospitals	0.9 per 100,000 persons
Health service coverage	70%
Mothers dying in childbirth	30 per 1,000 births
Women using contraception	10%
Under 5 mortality rate	108 per 1,000
Calorie consumption	87% of required intake (average)

Economy

GDP per capita	$1,000
GDP composition	39% agriculture, 17% industry, 44% services
Annual growth rate	7%
Military Expenditure	$550 million per annum
Exports	$1.7 billion
Imports	$1.2 billion
Debt	$24.9 billion

Sources: UNICEF, WHO, DFID, SID, CIA World Factbook 2001
All figures are the most recent published

WHY HAS SUDAN SUFFERED FAMINE?

Sudan is the largest country in Africa and is approximately the size of Europe. The Gezira is a fertile area near the banks of the River Nile. Much of the rest of the land is marginal which means that it is difficult to grow crops there. However, in the 1970s, not only did Sudan grow enough to feed itself, it produced a surplus that was exported.

How is it then that Sudan was described by UNICEF in June 2002 as "One of the six most at-risk countries in the Horn of Africa facing potential famine"? It was estimated that 600,000 people were at immediate risk of starvation. A combination of social, economic and political factors stretching back a number of years has resulted in a series of food crises leading to famine in the 1970s, the 1980s and the 1990s. There was a large-scale famine in 1998 when a massive aid operation was undertaken by the United Nations and a number of Non-governmental Agencies, such as Oxfam and Save the Children.

SOCIAL AND ECONOMIC FACTORS

A few rich merchants who also control the pricing and sale of grain own most of the good land. When these rich merchants expanded their grain growing business, many poor farmers lost their land for although they had been there for many years they did not have the legal documents to prove it.

There was also massive over-farming which lead to land exhaustion. Many vulnerable people had to leave the land and settle in shantytowns near big cities to try to find work. Drought made the problems worse in the 1980s with 90% of cattle dying. Without cattle, the rural people lost their traditional means of trade and exchange.

CIVIL WAR

POLITICAL FACTOR

Undoubtedly the civil war in Sudan has been a major cause of food shortages. In 1985 a group of military officers took over the government, establishing a fundamentalist Islamic state in 1989. Fighting continued with the Christian South. In a country where the average annual GDP is $1,000, the government spends $550 million on the armed forces. Many people are killed directly, but many more suffer the consequences of war.

The supply and distribution of food is seriously hampered by the effects of war. In 2002, UNICEF commented, "There are still too many children and families who are not receiving enough food." It is estimated by the International Famine Centre that 20–30% of food aid is diverted by armies for their own use.

Aid workers have come under attack, with a number being killed, injured, captured or beaten up by soldiers. In 2000, bombings in some areas caused the temporary halt of a major relief programme, Operation Lifeline Sudan. Many tens of thousands suffered or died as a result. Attacks on food distribution centres have also caused major problems.

Many children are forced to fight, becoming so-called 'child soldiers'. In addition to the physical dangers they face, many are deeply psychologically damaged as a result of their experiences. Economic growth was poor during the 1990s. A combination of the effects of war, extreme weather conditions and weak agricultural prices on the world market combined to create a poor economy.

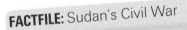

FACTFILE: Sudan's Civil War

* Sudan's civil war is the longest uninterrupted civil war in the world, having continued non-stop for seventeen years.

* More than 2 million Sudanese people have died from war-related causes.

* Around 4 million people have been uprooted from their homes and communities. 400,000 have fled as refugees to neighbouring countries.

* More than 1.2 million people are at risk of starvation in the South, which is at war with the Northern government. Drought has played a part, but the war is seen as the main cause.

* During the famine of 1991 the government prepared to step up the war and attacked forces in the South the following year.

* Violence and government blocking of food supplies were responsible for tens of thousands dying during the 1998 famine.

* In January 2002 a ceasefire agreement was signed, but fighting still goes on.

EYEWITNESS ACCOUNT

We saw a hungry Sudanese villager named Aguek gathering red ants that would be made into a soup for her family. Earlier this year she was starving while we in the West had huge food surpluses.

Parts of Sudan were in famine while others were producing an abundance of crops. Even within villages we witnessed considerable variations in the access of different families to food.

"This famine was man-made and the cause is war," said an aid worker. "This is definitely not a problem that can be blamed simply on lack of food."

Adapted *Irish Times* July 2001

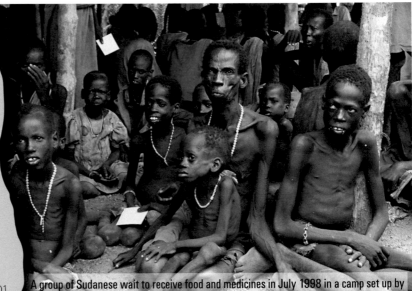

A group of Sudanese wait to receive food and medicines in July 1998 in a camp set up by UNICEF in Wau, southern Sudan. More than 60,000 people fled the region because of the civil war and wandered the streets of this city, malnourished and disoriented.

A SUMMARY OF SOCIAL, ECONOMIC AND POLITICAL PROBLEMS IN AFRICA

POPULATION GROWTH
In many areas the environment cannot sustain the increasing population. There is an increased demand for food that may not be able to be met. Land gets over-farmed causing even more problems.

EFFECTS OF WAR AND ARMED CONFLICTS
Life is disrupted, land cannot be farmed, money is diverted to pay for the military, aid workers cannot get through to the starving.

TYPE OF GOVERNMENT
Governments can be corrupt, diverting money to keep them in power, or to pay for a rich lifestyle.
The poor suffer while the rich benefit. Often money is spent on the military to keep the government in power.

POSITION OF WOMEN
Women do most of the agricultural work, but most are not allowed to own land, meaning that it is not farmed as well as it might be. Also, literacy rates for women are low which means that they are denied the skills and education that could help increase crop yields, or allow them to work in skilled, better paid work.

DEBT
Many countries owe billions of dollars in loans which they may never be able to pay back. Money is diverted from social projects like health and education to pay interest on loans.

POOR HEALTH AND HEALTH SERVICES
AIDS, malaria and many diseases that are inoculated against in the West are common in Africa. People die younger, they are often too weak to work and cannot get adequate medical treatment. Many children die before their fifth birthday.

POVERTY
The income of most people in African countries is too low to meet their needs.

ACTIVITIES

1 Provide evidence that Sudan is a country at risk of famine.

2 What social and economic factors contribute to food shortages in Sudan?

3 *Civil War – A Major Political Factor*
   a) Explain how civil war has contributed to food shortages.
   b) Study the Factfile on page 11 and describe the consequences of the civil war for the people of Sudan.

4 Read the Eyewitness Account and explain why the writer says, that the famine was "man-made".

5 Choose any four problems from the summary. Explain why you consider these to be the most important.

THE POLITICS OF AID
AID GIVEN BY DEVELOPED COUNTRIES TO AFRICA

What you will learn

1   The types of aid given to African countries.

2   What is meant by bilateral aid, multi-lateral aid and tired aid.

3   The ways in which the British government helps to meet the needs of some African countries.

WHAT IS AID?

Aid is help which can assist a country to overcome problems it faces. It can be long-term, short-term or medium-term. There are numerous types of aid but good aid focuses on the problems of a particular country then targets aid to solve problems by listening to the people who are suffering and responding to them. Increasingly, the slogan 'Trade not Aid' has been adopted as the best way of helping developing countries.

Aid comes from three main sources:

1   From the governments of developed nations.

2   From international organisations such as the United Nations. (See Section 4.)

3   From voluntary organisations such as Oxfam, Christian Aid, Save the Children etc.

FACTFILE: Types of Aid

Food Aid
Surplus food such as cereals, powdered milk, grain and dairy products can be sent. Often, food aid is part of emergency relief aid projects.

Financial Aid
This can involve loans of money which have to be paid back with interest; grants which do not have to be paid back; subsidies to assist exports; trade deals.

Equipment
Specialist equipment to aid development can be sent, such as vehicles, farming equipment, engineering parts, manufacturing equipment.

Emergency Relief Aid
This aid is sent to assist with disasters such as earthquakes, floods and droughts. By sending immediate assistance such as tents, medical supplies, food and clothing, short-term help is given to deal with immediate problems.

Specialist Workers and Experts
Teachers, trainers, medical professionals and specialist advisers can be sent. Researchers and managers are also useful as they can organise and plan training programmes.

Military Aid
To support a friendly government facing attack or the threat of attack, such things as guns, tanks, various other weapons, military advisers and peacekeeping forces can be sent.

BILATERL AID AND MULTILATERAL AID

All aid is either bilateral aid or multilateral aid. Bilateral aid is aid given by one country to another country. Multilateral aid is aid given by a group of countries, e.g. aid given by the United Nations (UN) or the European Union (EU). (See Figure 1.7.)

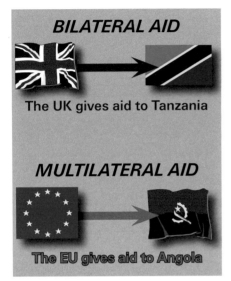

BILATERAL AID

The UK gives aid to Tanzania

MULTILATERAL AID

The EU gives aid to Angola

Figure 1.7

In 1984 the EU agreed the Dublin Plan. This gave aid to eight badly affected countries. By 1986, one-third of all aid given to sub-Saharan Africa came from EU members.

TIED AID

When bilateral aid is given, there are usually conditions attached. For example, a country in Africa may be given a grant from Britain, but in return a proportion of that money has to be spent on British goods and services. Such aid, therefore, has 'strings attached'. Hence it is referred to as tied aid. (Note: A grant of money does not have to be paid back; a loan has to be paid back with interest.) Sometimes tied aid is referred to as boomerang aid because, like a boomerang, it returns to the person who sent it. (See Figure 1.8.)

Boys in Sudan carry food aid from UNICEF. This is multilateral aid in action. The members of the UN give money to fund the United Nations. Part of this money is used to provide aid to countries in need.

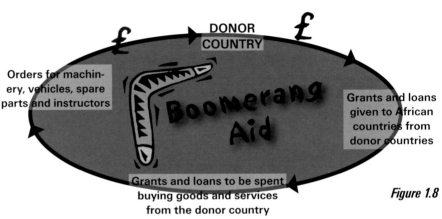

DONOR COUNTRY

Orders for machinery, vehicles, spare parts and instructors

Grants and loans given to African countries from donor countries

Grants and loans to be spent buying goods and services from the donor country

Figure 1.8

ACTIVITIES

1   Draw up and complete a table like the one below.
    Discuss this first with a partner, or as part of a group.

TYPE OF AID	ADVANTAGES	DISADVANTAGES
Financial aid		
Specialist workers		
Emergency relief aid		
Food aid		
Military aid		

2   Which two types of aid do you feel are the best long-term solutions? Give reasons for your answers.

3   Which two types of aid do you feel are the best for short-term solutions? Give reasons for your answers.

4   What is the difference between bilateral and multilateral aid?

5   Say if each of the following is an example of bilateral or multilateral aid.

    a)   The USA sends tractors to Ethiopia.
    b)   The UN sends medical supplies to Rwanda.
    c)   The EU agrees to send surplus grain to Mozambique.
    d)   France sends doctors to Senegal.
    e)   A group of Scandinavian countries agrees to send farming experts to Gabon.

Focus on *TIED AID*

act!onaid

Action Aid is a Non-governmental Organisation (NGO), which works to eliminate poverty in developing countries. It is highly critical of tied aid. The main criticisms which have been identified are:

➤ Spending on goods and services takes place in the country that gave the aid, not in the country receiving it.

➤ It favours companies in the donor country rather than in the country receiving the aid.

➤ It can distort programmes or result in them being ineffective thereby increasing the costs.

➤ It does not promote sustainable development and can lead to wasteful practices.

➤ It discourages local companies and businesses from participating.

➤ It results in an over-reliance on the knowledge, technology and spare parts of companies in the developed countries.

CHANGING ATTITUDES TO AID

Governments around the world have recently acknowledged the criticisms made of tied aid. Three changes took place in 2001–2002.

● Firstly, the Organisation for Economic Cooperation and Development (OECD), made up of twenty two developed countries, reached an agreement to eliminate tied aid. In May 2001, the OECD announced that its members would offer aid without requiring the country receiving the aid to use the money given to buy from suppliers in the donor country. The OECD explained that this policy covered half of the $8,000 billion a year given by its members in aid.

● Secondlly, in 2001, the European Union (EU) stated that it would support the OECD agreement, but only in relation to the world's forty eight least developed countries. In response, Clare Short, the UK Minister responsible for overseas aid said, "I am disappointed by Commissioner Neilson's stand on untying. The concession is still only for untying aid to the least developed countries."

● Thirdly, in May 2002 the British government announced the end of tied aid. An Act will be passed which will make this law.

UK Government has tied aid to water project in Ghana

Christian Aid has learned that the Department For International Development (DFID) has used £10 million of aid money to help persuade the government of Ghana to lease part of its water supply to foreign companies.

Mark Curtis of Christian Aid said, "The UK government claims it has ended tied aid. However, aid money is being made available on the condition that two foreign companies will sign leases to run water supplies for ten years." This move could see the cost of drinking water rise by up to 300%.

Four companies will bid for the contract including one from the UK.

Adapted news article from Christian Aid website, 2 November 2002

British Prime Minister Tony Blair and International Development Minister Clare Short meet cocoa farmers on a cocoa co-operative farm in Nankesi, eastern Ghana during their four day visit to west Africa.

AIMS OF DFID

1 To cut in half the proportion of people living in extreme poverty by 2015.

2 To provide basic health care and access to primary education for all in developing countries.

3 To work in partnership with governments that are committed to meeting the aims of the department.

4 To work with multilateral agencies such as the United Nations, the European Union and the World Bank.

5 To deliver benefits to the poorest people in the countries targeted.

ACTIVITIES _____

1 What is tied aid?

2 What criticisms have been made of tied aid?

3 In what ways have the attitudes of some developed countries changed towards tied aid?

4 What criticisms have been made of UK aid to Tanzania and Ghana?

HOW THE UNITED KINGDOM HELPS TO MEET THE NEEDS OF AFRICAN COUNTRIES

In the UK, the Department for International Development (DFID) is responsible for all bilateral aid funded by the government. This department was established in 1997 when New Labour won the General Election. DFID replaced the Overseas Development Agency (ODA). The government has also introduced the New Partnership for African Development (Nepad), which demands that African countries tackle corruption and act in a democratic and fair way as a condition of getting aid.

The Labour government has increased the budget available to DFID, strengthened it and made clear that it will increase its commitment to development in areas such as Africa. Clare Short is the Minister responsible for overseas development and as such is responsible for DFID. In an article in May 2002, she said about aid, "It is morally right that we help those who are hungry. People must not die of hunger when there is so much food in the world. People must not be punished because their government is corrupt."

In 2001 the UK budget for overseas development was £3,235 million, which represents 0.32% of GNI (formerly known as GNP). This was an increase of 6% in real terms. The amount spent by the DFID remained the same. On 25 June 2002, Prime Minister Tony Blair announced at a conference in Canada that his intention was to increase bilateral aid to Africa to £1 billion by 2006 from the present £632 million.

UK government under fire despite policy changes

Tanzania radar deal under fire

Andrew Pendleton, from the charity Christian Aid, today criticised a UK deal to supply a radar system to Tanzania. It is claimed that the system is more expensive than it should be for the country's needs. It is also claimed it is a system that is out of date.

Mr Pendleton said, "Although there is no suggestion of tied aid, the decision has re-kindled familiar claims that profits are being put before tackling poverty."

The affair reminds critics of a report published by the Treasury in 1996 which found that UK firms had overcharged recipients of British tied aid by as much as 50% for shovels and hoes. Prices for British buses were overpriced by 25% and 27% for water pumps.

Adapted from BBC News website June 2002

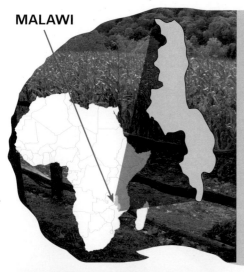

MALAWI

FOOD SHORTAGE CRISIS IN MALAWI

In May 2002, DFID was at the forefront of tackling the food shortage crisis in Malawi. There was a substantial shortfall in the maize harvest due to prolonged drought, resulting in large-scale food shortages. £5.1 million was provided in food relief. In addition, DFID workers cooperated with the government of Malawi in drawing up a food security plan.

Seeds and fertiliser had been distributed in November 2001 to 1 million of the poorest farming families to reduce dependency on food handouts. Without this assistance the crisis in 2002 would have been even worse.

BILATERAL AID
Top 20 Recipient Countries

COUNTRY	£M
India	117
Uganda	86
Ghana	73
Bangladesh	73
Tanzania	69
Malawi	57
Zambia	56
Kenya	52
Mozambique	41
Sierra Leone	35
Rwanda	33
States of Yugoslavia	32
South Africa	30
China	30
Russian Federation	26
Montserrat	21
Indonesia	20
Nepal	18
Nigeria	17
Ethiopia	16
Total for top 20 recipient countries	902
Total for all countries	1,414
Proportion of total to top 20	64%

African countries

Table 1.2

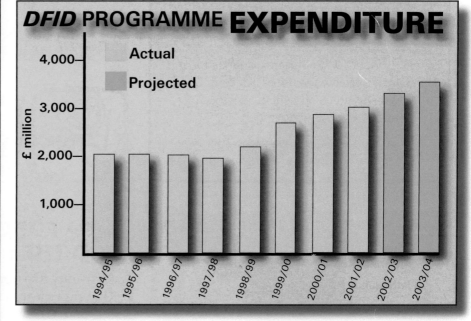

Figure 1.9

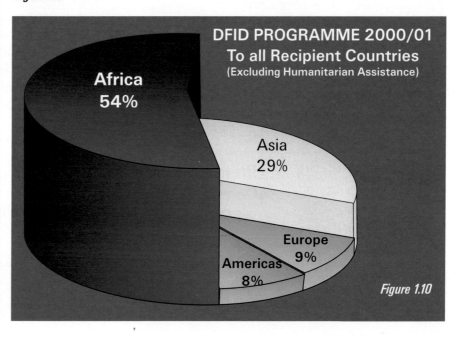

Figure 1.10

1 Study Table 1.2.

*"Similar levels of aid are given
to most of the countries in the table."*
                                    View of an official.

Explain why the official could be accused of exaggeration.

2 Study Figure 1.9. Provide evidence to support the view that "DFID spending increased in 2001–2002, and is predicted to rise in the future."

3 Study Figure 1.10. From the data, what conclusions can be drawn regarding how DFID aid is spent?

4 Study Figure 1.11. What conclusions can be reached regarding where DFID aid is allocated?

5 Study Figure 1.12. Provide evidence for and against the view that "the UK's contribution to overseas development is generous in comparison to other countries."

4 What conclusions can be made about American aid, now and in the future?

DFID PROGRAMME
Major Forms of Aid

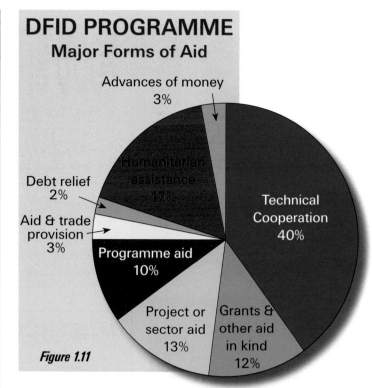

Advances of money 3%
Humanitarian assistance 17%
Debt relief 2%
Aid & trade provision 3%
Programme aid 10%
Technical Cooperation 40%
Project or sector aid 13%
Grants & other aid in kind 12%

Figure 1.11

Focus on *US aid*

USA FOREIGN AID THE LOWEST

Of twenty two developed countries, the USA ranks last in foreign aid as a percentage of GNI. America devotes just 0.1% of its wealth to foreign aid which is less than half the rich nations' average.

It is said that so little is given because it is not a vote winner for politicians. Studies, however, indicate that there could be more support than was previously assumed.

Researchers at the University of Maryland found that voters thought that the government was giving about 20% of GNI in foreign aid, rather than the reality of 0.1%. Voters thought 20% was too much, but felt that 10% would be more appropriate. The researchers concluded that voters were receptive to the idea of increasing foreign aid.

Adapted from *Calendar Live* 27 May 2001

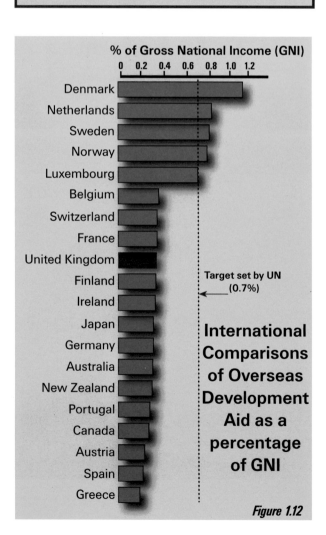

% of Gross National Income (GNI)
0   0.2   0.4   0.6   0.8   1.0   1.2

Denmark
Netherlands
Sweden
Norway
Luxembourg
Belgium
Switzerland
France
United Kingdom
Finland
Ireland
Japan
Germany
Australia
New Zealand
Portugal
Canada
Austria
Spain
Greece

**Target set by UN
(0.7%)**

International Comparisons of Overseas Development Aid as a percentage of GNI

Figure 1.12

TANZANIA

SOCIAL AND ECONOMIC PROFILE

One-party rule came to an end in 1995 with the first democratic elections held since the 1970s. Tanzania is now a multi-party democracy. The head of government is President Benjamin Mkapa. All citizens aged eighteen and over may vote in elections.

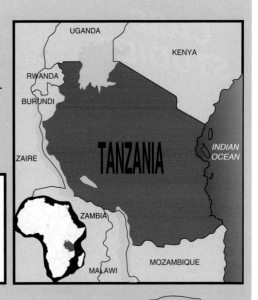

Population	36,232,074
Population growth	2.61%
Infant mortality	79.41 deaths per 1000 live births
Life expectancy	51.04 years (male)
	52.95 years (female)
People living with AIDS/HIV	1.3 million

AIMS OF UK AID TO TANZANIA

- To improve the economy.

- To improve education, particularly for the poor.

- To improve health, particularly for the poor.

- To improve job opportunities, particularly for the poor.

- To improve the opportunities to participate in the process of development, particularly for the poor.

PAST, PRESENT AND FUTURE PROJECTS INCLUDE THE FOLLOWING:

● Improving access for poorer people to markets and services.

● Working to sustain the environment and improve the land for the future by community-based approaches.

● Agricultural research to improve cattle production and the use of land.

● Improving and maintaining the road network which will help to develop the economy.

● Improving access to safe water, focusing on rural areas and smaller towns. Linked to this will be the promotion of good hygiene practices and improved sanitation. In 2002 only 50% of the population had access to safe water. Diseases causing diarrhoea are currently one of the main causes of child mortality.

● Supporting new laws introduced by the Tanzanian government to allow decisions to be taken at local government level rather than by central government.

● Major causes of illness and death will be targeted including malaria, HIV/AIDS. Major strengthening of child health services will be a priority including immunisation and the eradication of polio.

DFID is committed to working closely with the government of Tanzania and with other groups giving aid. The project began in 1997 with a goal of reducing by 50% the proportion of Tanzanians living in poverty by 2015. The estimated expenditure for the year 2001–2002 was £63 million. Since 1997 the average spent each year has been £54 million.

How aid took Tanzania to the classroom

Four years ago, Monica's parents died. She went to live with her aunt, Mwajuma who could not afford the 5,000 Tanzanian shillings a year (£3.50) to send her niece to school. However, she had heard of the new scheme, partly funded by DFID, giving free primary education to all. This year, £45 million of DFID money went into the scheme.

The family is so poor that it lives entirely on maize porridge, but with her education Monica has hope that she will get a good job when she is older. There are tens of thousands of children like Monica.

CASE STUDIES

Scourge of Malaria

New wells in Tanzania have had a big positive impact on people's health, but malaria still remains a major problem. Olipa Chilemela explains, "I had eleven children, but now I have nine. They died of malaria as did three of my grandchildren."

Now Olipa has mosquito nets for her family thanks to a DFID scheme which subsidises the cost of manufacturing the nets. However, even at a price of £1.80 they are proving too expensive for the very poor.

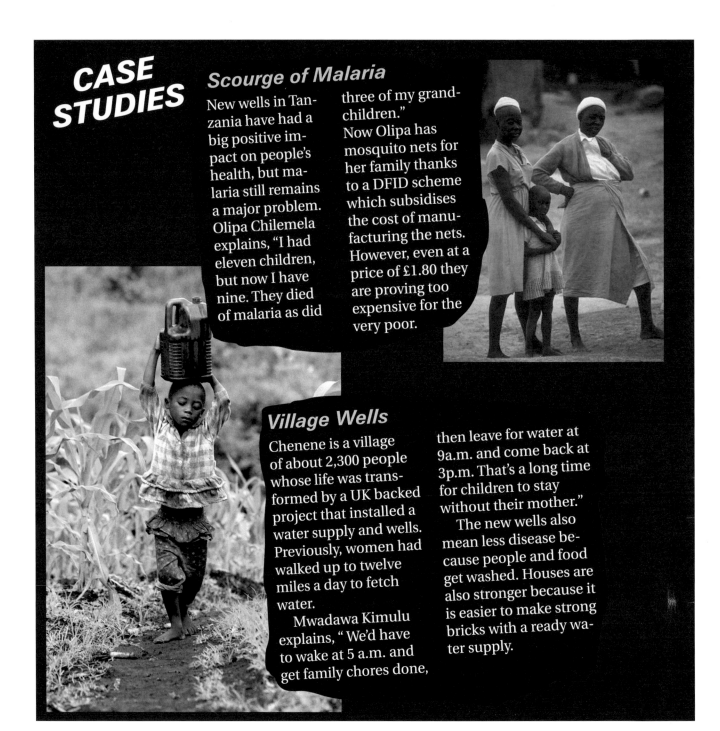

Village Wells

Chenene is a village of about 2,300 people whose life was transformed by a UK backed project that installed a water supply and wells. Previously, women had walked up to twelve miles a day to fetch water.

Mwadawa Kimulu explains, "We'd have to wake at 5 a.m. and get family chores done, then leave for water at 9a.m. and come back at 3p.m. That's a long time for children to stay without their mother."

The new wells also mean less disease because people and food get washed. Houses are also stronger because it is easier to make strong bricks with a ready water supply.

ACTIVITIES

1   Read the Profile of Tanzania and Aims of UK aid to Tanzania, then answer the following questions:
    a)   What are Tanzania's major needs?
    b)   Choose five examples of UK aid to Tanzania and explain why the aid would benefit the country.

2   Explain how the following DFID projects have helped people in Tanzania:
    a)   Education
    b)   Village wells.

3   Why has the mosquito net scheme not been a complete success?

THE POLITICS OF AID
HOW THE UN HELPS TO MEET THE NEEDS OF AFRICAN COUNTRIES

In June 1945, the aims of the United Nations (UN) were established. Fifty countries signed the charter which set out the aims of the UN. Each country promised to abide by the aims when it signed the UN Charter.

The key idea guiding the formation of the UN was to provide a forum whereby nations of the world could work together and cooperate to improve the conditions of people in the world.

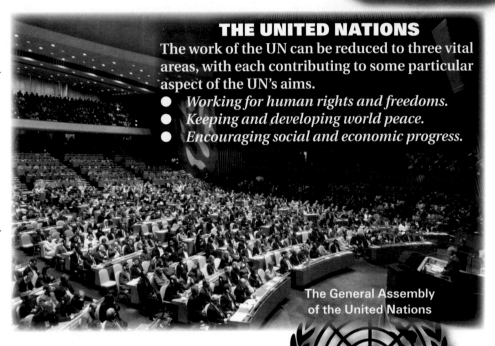

THE UNITED NATIONS

The work of the UN can be reduced to three vital areas, with each contributing to some particular aspect of the UN's aims.

● *Working for human rights and freedoms.*
● *Keeping and developing world peace.*
● *Encouraging social and economic progress.*

The General Assembly of the United Nations

UNITED NATIONS SPECIALISED AGENCIES

In order to meet its aims and principles, the United Nations works through a series of Specialised Agencies. Each has special skills and expertise to help meet the needs of developing nations. The Specialised Agencies which can be of most help to developing countries are listed below.

● The International Labour Organisation (ILO)

● The Food and Agricuture Organisation (FAO)

● The World Health Organisation (WHO)

● United Nations Children's Fund (UNICEF)

● United Nations Educational, Scientific and Cultural Organisation (UNESCO)

FACTFILE: The WHO

The World Health Organisation is there to meet medical needs by promoting good health and good medical facilities. The WHO has been involved in numerous projects in Africa which have included the following:

● Helping governments to set up health services.

● Training health professionals such as doctors, nurses, midwives and health visitors.

● Developing primary health care at local village level where hospitals and doctors are not readily available.

● Researching and working on health problems, eg. AIDS.

● Mass immunisation campaigns.

FACTFILE: The ILO

The ILO is concerned with trying to improve working conditions. Frequently in African countries wages are low, safety conditions are poor and workers, often children, are exploited. The ILO has been involved in addressing the following:

- Improving conditions of work and attempting to improve health and safety.
- Helping young children who may be forced to work for over twelve hours a day.
- Researching conditions and offering models of good practice to those who run factories and businesses.

FACTFILE: The FAO

The FAO specialises in trying to raise levels of nutrition and in working on methods of improving the food supply by farmers. African projects have included the following:

- Helping governments to train people to work on programmes aimed at improving crop yields, nutrition and the quality of crops.
- Researching and developing farming methods which can be applied to local conditions.
- Such projects have involved new irrigation schemes, using high yield crops, applying appropriate fertilisers and developing fisheries, forestry and cattle farming.
- Introducing new knowledge, equipment and modern methods of farming.
- Supplying experts, advisers and educators.

FACTFILE: UNESCO

UNESCO is concerned with developing education in its broadest possible sense. As well as attempting to improve literacy levels, other areas such as science and the arts are promoted. Projects in Africa have included:

- Encouraging governments to establish education systems which are compulsory for all.
- Sending advisers and teachers/lecturers to help create high quality schooling.
- Carrying out research in areas such as education, science and communication.
- Working to save works of art, monuments, areas of historic interest and the dying culture and social systems of tribal groups.
- Encouraging cooperation in arts and culture between African countries and the rest of the world.

FACTFILE: UNICEF

UNICEF's function is to help children in need, and also to help the mothers of these children. It focuses on a variety of different areas which include the following:

- Organising emergency relief for children after a disaster.
- Working with WHO to set up medical facilities and programmes such as immunisation, birth control advice or establishing health centres.

- Projects to help mother and child such as their breast-feeding campaign, education campaigns and safe motherhood campaigns.
- School projects to lower the high rates of illiteracy in many African countries.

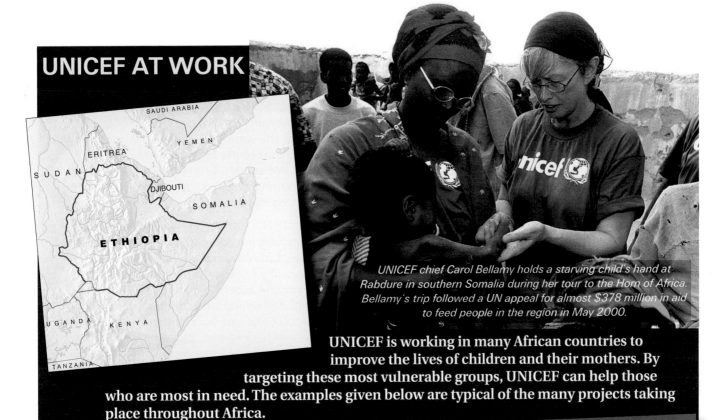

UNICEF AT WORK

UNICEF chief Carol Bellamy holds a starving child's hand at Rabdure in southern Somalia during her tour to the Horn of Africa. Bellamy's trip followed a UN appeal for almost $378 million in aid to feed people in the region in May 2000.

UNICEF is working in many African countries to improve the lives of children and their mothers. By targeting these most vulnerable groups, UNICEF can help those who are most in need. The examples given below are typical of the many projects taking place throughout Africa.

ACTION IN ETHIOPIA

Since 1999, food has been distributed to drought affected regions. Fifty feeding stations have been set up to give nutrition to children who are severely malnourished. The Gode area in the south-eastern region was particularly targeted in 2001 because child malnutrition rates there were some of the highest in the country.

A training programme has been set up to teach health workers how to care for severely malnourished women and children.

From January 2002, high numbers of cases of meningitis have been reported. In response, UNICEF has launched a vaccination campaign to deliver 500,000 doses of vaccine to combat this problem.

In 2001 mass vaccinations to eradicate polio were introduced with 14 million children being given injections. In addition, measles and malaria were targeted. 180 tons of medical supplies were airlifted to prepare for the winter dry season of 2001–2002.

Water and sanitation projects have been set up benefiting over 850,000 people. Throughout 2000 and beyond, shelter and food have been provided for families forced to flee the war-torn regions of Tigray and Afar in the North-east.

Landmine awareness campaigns have been established in the region since 2000.

ACTION IN SUDAN

UNICEF is working to increase access to safe drinking water. Water pumps are being repaired and wells are being dug. Repairing hand pumps alone benefited over 500,000 people in 2001.

In response to drought, programmes have been established in the states of Darfur and Kordofan focusing on water and sanitation, improving health, and helping to meet the educational needs of around 900,000 children.

Landmines, which are a result of the continuing civil war, cause widespread injury and death. The Sudanese government has estimated that more than 700,000 people have had limbs amputated as a consequence of landmine explosions. Thirty landmine awareness workshops have been set up, reaching 4,500 of those most at risk in 2000.

CASE STUDY: UNICEF in Mozambique

UNICEF Official

Mozambique is one of the poorest countries in the world. It is still recovering from a bitter war and has recently been hit by floods that caused further problems. We at UNICEF are involved in a major series of programmes to strengthen and support the country in meeting its basic needs.

We are working in cooperation with the government of Mozambique. We have agreed that together we will work to improve conditions for women and children, increase access to good quality social services and strengthen families' and communities' abilities to protect and care for children.

We are involved in many projects and the following will give an idea of what we are doing. I am involved in developing children's rights. There are many children orphaned because their parents have died of AIDS. We estimate that there will be 1,133,209 such orphans by 2007. Many children are neglected, exploited and abused, or left to look after themselves.

Our education programme is very important. We are working with the government to ensure that all children between 6 and 12 years will have access to a high standard of education. Currently only 44% of boys and 36% of girls enrol in primary school. Our plan aims to provide primary education for every child by 2006.

The health programme focuses on reducing infant death rates, eliminating polio and tetanus and reducing measles by 90%. We have also set targets to immunise up to 80% of children against common diseases, improve health education and to increase health services to reach 60% from the 1994 figure of 40%. We are also working to improve sanitation and water supplies.

Mozambique

Mozambique

I am an orphan. My parents died of AIDS two years ago. UNICEF has made a great difference to my life. I lived on the streets for two years and earned a little money helping out a stallholder in the market. He often beat me and kicked me. I was given the rotten or bruised fruit to eat, but in the end I ran away because he was so cruel.

I used to sleep where I could and suffered from all sorts of diseases and other health problems. I had no doctor to treat me and no one to care for my health.

UNICEF has made a big difference to my life. I now go to school where I also get a free healthy meal. I also have a place to sleep with a family in my old community. I get regular health check-ups and have been immunised against a range of dangerous diseases. The water in the area where I live is now fresh and we have good sanitation, which reduces the risk of disease.

Sipho's Story

ACTIVITIES

Refer to pages 21 and 22.

1 Which UN Specialised Agency or Agencies could help to deal with the following problems?

a) Overfarmed land

b) Poor farming methods

c) High rates of illiteracy

d) An outbreak of polio

e) Dangerous machinery in a fruit-picking factory

f) Starving children

2 Which two Specialised Agencies do you consider could be of most help to countries in Africa? Give detailed reasons for your answer.

Study pages 23 and 24.

3 Under the following headings describe how UNICEF has helped to meet the needs of African people:

– UNICEF in Sudan

– UNICEF in Ethiopia

– UNICEF in Mozambique

4 In what ways has UNICEF improved Sipho's life?

5 Design a leaflet in which your aim is to publicise the work done by UNICEF in Africa.

The summary of the work of the Food and Agriculture Organisation on page 22 outlines the general areas in which this Specialised Agency gets involved. The FAO plays a major part in helping to meet the needs of many countries in Africa. The following three case studies highlight some of the projects designed to do this.

FAO case study 1

AFRICA LAND AND WATER INITIATIVE

This project was begun in 2001 and will run until 2004. The project will cost $2,490,000,000. The aim of this project is to provide African countries with opportunities to manage land and water resources. By doing this, social, economic and environmental benefits should follow.

Water is a major resource, necessary to continue developing agriculture which accounts for 34% of Africa's GDP, 70% of its labour force and 40% of its exports, but presently it is under threat.

Water supplies are not being managed well in many cases and the FAO is working with governments and other agencies to overcome this problem. Major projects are under way in the African countries of Niger, Nigeria, Chad and the Volta Basin area.

Supplies of water are being made available to the poor, and businesses which pollute water supplies are being made to pay compensation. Experts are working with local people to manage water supplies better and to provide the skills and tools necessary to do this. Grants, loans and aid packages are being made available to improve water supplies and ensure that they are well managed for long-term use by future generations.

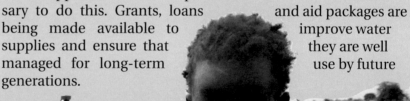

Grain being picked in a watered field.

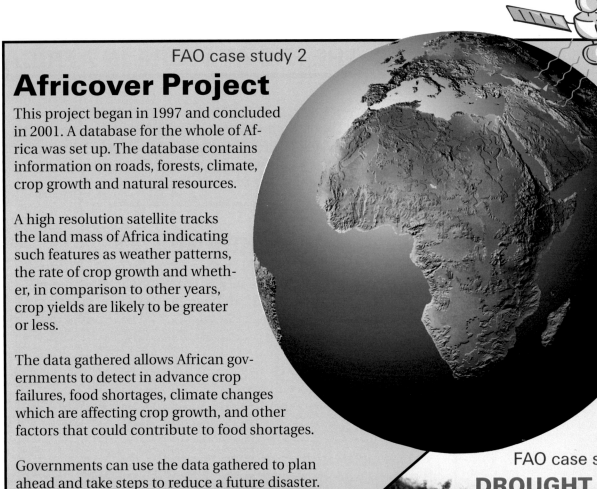

Africover Project

This project began in 1997 and concluded in 2001. A database for the whole of Africa was set up. The database contains information on roads, forests, climate, crop growth and natural resources.

A high resolution satellite tracks the land mass of Africa indicating such features as weather patterns, the rate of crop growth and whether, in comparison to other years, crop yields are likely to be greater or less.

The data gathered allows African governments to detect in advance crop failures, food shortages, climate changes which are affecting crop growth, and other factors that could contribute to food shortages.

Governments can use the data gathered to plan ahead and take steps to reduce a future disaster.

FAO case study 3
DROUGHT AND DESERTIFICATION CONTROL

For many years the FAO has been at the forefront of improving land in Africa which has suffered from drought, locust invasions, and desertification (fertile land being turned into desert as a result of bad farming, cutting down trees which allows the soil to wash away, or the creeping nature of the desert itself which engulfs land as it endlessly moves).

The FAO is working with the governments of Burkino Faso, Cape Verde, Niger, Senegal and other African countries to make better use of land and control desertification. In addition, it is working to rehabilitate land in order to make it suitable for farming again. Work is being undertaken to ensure that water supplies do not dry up.

Shown are Eucalyptus saplings that have been planted to prevent soil erosion near Lompoul, Senegal.

The WFP is the United Nation's agency most involved in combating hunger in Africa. It has been in operation since 1963 and is without doubt the world's largest international food aid organisation. More than this, however, the WFP aims to address the causes of food shortages.

World Food Programme

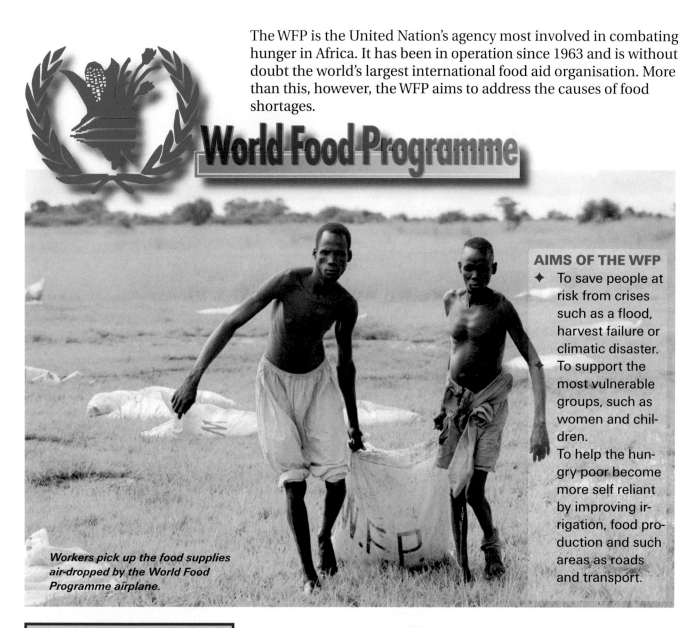

Workers pick up the food supplies air-dropped by the World Food Programme airplane.

AIMS OF THE WFP

✦ To save people at risk from crises such as a flood, harvest failure or climatic disaster.

✦ To support the most vulnerable groups, such as women and children.

✦ To help the hungry poor become more self reliant by improving irrigation, food production and such areas as roads and transport.

ACTIVITIES

1. Imagine you are a United Nations field worker. Write a report for your project manager in the United Nations headquarters in New York, explaining:

   ● the problems of water supply
   ● the importance of good water supplies
   ● what the FAO is achieving
   ● your view of how good the aid will be.

2. What is the Africover Project?

3. What is the FAO doing to improve land in African countries?

FACTFILE: The WFP

◆ Over the last thirty eight years the WFP has become the world's largest provider of free school meals.

◆ In the year 2000, more than twelve million children were fed in schools in fifty four countries.

◆ The WFP is one of the world leaders in promoting education for girls. Part of this scheme involves giving a month's free food rations to the parents of girls enrolled in school. This has resulted in an increase in the enrolment of girls of up to 300% in some areas.

◆ In Kenya, Uganda and Zambia, the WFP has put in place feeding programmes for war orphans and HIV/AIDS orphans.

◆ For an average of only 12p a day, or £21 a year, a child can be fed in school for a year.

Targeting Micronutrient Malnutrition

WFP worker

Micronutrient malnutrition is a lack of iron, iodine, and vitamin A. The WFP has introduced the production of Indiamix which is a blended food that is produced from materials readily available in African countries, such as wheat and soy.

A simple 100 gram ration provides 80–90% of the recommended allowance of essential micronutrients. The WFP has introduced Indiamix to the African countries of Malawi, Eritrea, Ethiopia, Kenya and Senegal.

How does Indiamix help where it is used?

Four out of ten childhood deaths are prevented.

The number of women dying during childbirth drops by more than a third.

The work rate of people increases by up to 40%.

The ability to learn increases.

GDP has increased by up to 5%.

Case Study – **The Benefits of Food Aid in Schools**

Providing nutritious food at school has been found to be a very simple but very effective way of getting children in Africa to attend school. In many African countries literacy rates are very low, especially for girls. Education is one way of breaking the cycle of poverty, by making people more self-reliant and employable.

A UNESCO survey showed that in countries with an adult literacy rate of around 40%, per capita GNI averaged $210 while in countries with at least 80% literacy rates, the annual per capita GNI was at least $1,000.

Illiterate girls are married as young as 11 years of age in some African countries and may have up to seven children before the age of 18. However, girls who are educated marry later, and have an average of 50% fewer children.

WFP worker

Where women have been educated there has been a 50% drop in child malnutrition. Clearly then, something as simple as getting children to attend school can have an enormous impact on the lives, health and prosperity of people in African countries.

Children from the Lusala Primary School, Ludewa District, Tanzania.

FACTFILE: School Feeding in Action

➤ Where school meals are provided, enrolment and attendance at school increases greatly.

➤ A child who is fed is able to learn and concentrate better.

➤ Where take-home rations of food are provided, girls who would normally have to stay at home and work are given the opportunity by their families to learn.

➤ When an emergency happens and schools cannot operate normally, school feeding provides nutrition and education continues in whatever way possible.

ACTIVITIES

1. What are the aims of the WFP?

2. Study the WFP Factfile. Give three examples of work done by the WFP.

3. a) What is Indiamix?
   b) How does it help people in Africa?

4. Provide evidence to support the WFP worker's view that *"Education is one way of breaking the cycle of poverty."*

5. How can feeding programmes help to meet the needs of African people?

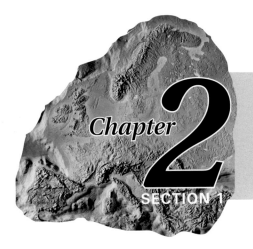

ECONOMIC ALLIANCES FROM COMMON MARKET TO EUROPEAN UNION

What you will learn:

1   How the European Union grew and developed.

2   The aims of the European Union.

3   The structure of the European Union.

THE FORMATION AND GROWTH OF THE EUROPEAN UNION

The European Union (EU) is the modern name for an organisation which started as the European Coal and Steel Community (ECSC) in 1951. The ECSC originally had six members who agreed to cooperate with regard to coal and steel production. In 1957 they signed two more treaties setting up the European Atomic Energy Commission (EURATOM) and the European Economic Community. As the Community widened its powers, the word 'Economic' was dropped from the title, and the organisation became simply the European Community. This term was changed again in the mid-1990s to the European Union.

The origins of the European Union lie in the desire of

politicians in the late 1940s to avoid another war in Europe. They saw the destruction caused by two major wars and wanted to make sure that such a thing could never happen again. The key was to make the major countries of Europe—especially France and Germany—depend on each other for economic stability.

POPULATION OF THE EUROPEAN UNION (million)	
Original Members (1957)	
Belgium	10
France	57
Germany	80
Italy	58
Luxembourg	0.4
Netherlands	15
Joined 1973	
Denmark	5
Ireland	4
United Kingdom	57
Joined 1981	
Greece	10
Joined 1986	
Portugal	10
Spain	40
Joined 1995	
Austria	8
Finland	5
Sweden	9
Total population	368.4

Members of the European Union (2003)

The European Union has a larger population than the United States of America, or the former Soviet Union, making it one of the most powerful political groupings in the world. More countries are set to join within the next ten years.

In 1957 the six members of the ECSC signed the Treaty of Rome, creating the European Economic Community. Its aim was to establish a 'Common Market' to develop and encourage trade between Community members and to improve living standards throughout all the countries of the Community.

The Treaty of Rome was a Customs Union. Once goods were within the Community they could be traded quite freely between countries with no taxes or duties applied. However, the Community could agree to impose taxes on goods entering from outside. In this way the member countries could protect their own industries and allow them to prosper, improving living standards within the borders of the Community.

Summary of the Aims of the European Union

- To encourage cooperation between member countries and so reduce the chance of conflict in Europe. If countries depend on each other then they cannot afford to fight!

- To improve living standards and working conditions throughout Europe.

- To improve trade links between members, and between the European Union and the rest of the world. The Cotonou Agreement is a treaty linking the European Union to Third World countries.

- To even out living standards across Europe, bringing poorer areas up to the standard of the better off regions.

- To achieve an ever closer relationship between the peoples of Europe, including freedom of movement for workers and students across the member countries.

- Harmonisation of laws and regulations across all member countries.

- To extend the Single European Currency (Euro) to all member countries.

HOW ARE DECISIONS TAKEN?

There are four main Institutions of the European Union.

The Council of the European Union

This body makes most of the major decisions. It also coordinates the economic policies of member states and shares control of the budget with the European Parliament. The Council is made up of one government Minister from each member state. The Minister who goes to meetings is appropriate to the main topics on the agenda. Sometimes Council will consist of all the Agriculture Ministers; on other occasions it will be made up of the Prime Ministers from each member country. Voting takes place using the Qualified Majority system. Larger countries have more power than smaller countries. The Presidency of the Council rotates around the member countries for six month periods.

The Commission

This is the Civil Service of the European Union. Commis-

sioners make suggestions about policy, but their main job is to put the decisions of the Council of the EU into practice.

The European Parliament

This is a directly elected assembly based in Strasbourg. The 626 Members (MEPs) serve five-year terms of office. Elections for the European Parliament are due to take place in 2004 and 2009. The Parliament makes comments on draft laws and sends proposed changes to the Council of the European Union. The photograph shows the MEPs voting in the chamber.

The European Court of Justice

This settles disputes about European Union law. Individual citizens can appeal to the Court if they feel that they have been unfairly treated.

Budgets

Fisheries

Regional Policy, Transport and Tourism

Development and Cooperation

Employment and Social Affairs

Legal Affairs and the Internal Market

Women's Rights and Equal Opportunities

Citizens' Freedoms and Rights, Justice and Home Affairs

Agriculture and Rural Development

EUROPEAN PARLIAMENT COMMITTEES The European Parliament has a total of seventeen committees. These look at the various aspects of the work of the European Union, and suggest changes to laws before they are approved by the Council of the EU.

Constitutional Affairs

Foreign Affairs, Human Rights and Defence

Budgetary Control

Environment, Public Health and Consumer Policy

Industry, External Trade, Research and Energy

Culture, Youth, Media, Education and Sport

Petitions

Economic and Monetary Affairs

ACTIVITIES

1 Why did countries such as France and Germany want to form a European Union in the 1950s?

2 *"The Treaty of Rome was a Customs Union."*
What is a Customs Union?

3 Briefly describe the powers and functions of the Council of the EU, the Commission and the European Parliament.

4 Which part of the European Union makes the final decisions?

5 What important issues are debated by the European Parliament Committees?

6 What are the main aims of the European Union?

MAKING THE LAWS IN THE EU

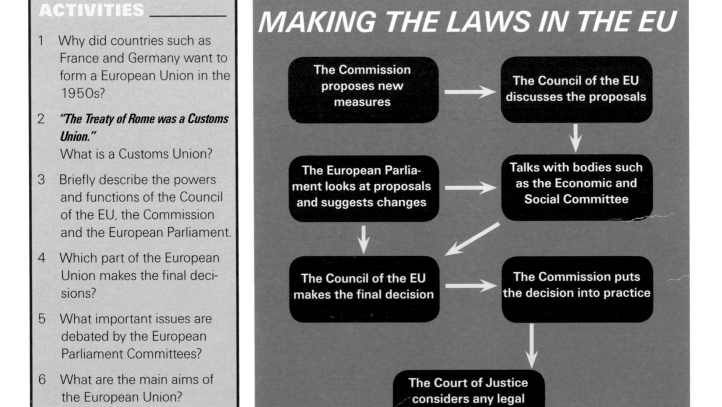

The Commission proposes new measures

The Council of the EU discusses the proposals

The European Parliament looks at proposals and suggests changes

Talks with bodies such as the Economic and Social Committee

The Council of the EU makes the final decision

The Commission puts the decision into practice

The Court of Justice considers any legal problems

Figure 2.1

FROM MAASTRICHT TO NICE

During the 1970s and 1980s most of the countries in the European Community were moving towards a closer economic, monetary and political union. The so-called 'federalists', including Jacques Delors, then President of the European Commission, wanted to 'deepen' the ties between existing members of the Community.

The 1991 Maastricht Treaty came out of this idea. An Inter-Governmental Conference was held in the Dutch town of Maastricht in December 1991.

The Maastricht Treaty had to be ratified by each member state. This meant that they had to get approval from their own Parliaments. Denmark, France and Ireland held referenda to ratify the Treaty, while other countries debated it in their Parliaments. The crucial point about the Maastricht Treaty was that it extended the scope of the European Union into new areas. Policies which used to be controlled by individual governments were now under the influence of Brussels.

There was considerable criticism of the Maastricht Treaty in Britain. Sections of the Conservative Party, in particular, were opposed to it. The criticisms which were made are summarised below.

✘ Individual countries lose identity as power is switched from national governments to the EU.

✘ Too much power is given to the EU institutions such as the Commission, which are undemocratic in the first place.

✘ Unacceptable common laws are imposed over a huge area. They do not take account of the different cultures, traditions and peoples living in these areas.

✘ Social policies which demand high wages and improved working conditions may force manufacturing out of Europe and into the low-wage economies of the developing world.

REPORT CARD
The 1991 Maastricht Treaty

AIM	PROGRESS
To create a European Union of states, building upon the European Community's existing provisions.	The EU has become stronger, with fewer major disputes between member states.
To create an area without borders, where no EU members would require passports.	In 1995 the Schengen Agreement was implemented, removing all border controls between member states. (The UK and Ireland stayed out of the agreement.)
To strengthen economic and social cooperation.	There is greater cross-national cooperation. The EU's social agenda on employment and equality was adopted at the Nice Summit.
To link the economic and financial affairs of all the EU countries.	The establishment of the European Central Bank, located in Frankfurt, was a major step towards economic and financial union.
To create one European currency.	In January 2002 eleven member states abolished their own currencies and introduced the EURO.
To share a common foreign and security policy.	The EU has adopted a higher profile on defence and security issues such as Yugoslavia and Global Terrorism.
To introduce citizenship of the European Union.	The idea of EU citizenship is still some time away. However, there has been convergence in terms of documentation and legal procedures.
To develop close cooperation in justice and home affairs.	Issues such as immigration and asylum seekers have led to some disagreements between member states.

The Nice Treaty

The Nice Treaty, agreed in December 2000, set the agenda for the European Union for the first ten years of the new millennium.

The main points of the Nice Treaty are listed below.

☆ Make preparations for enlarging EU membership to twenty seven countries.

☆ Strengthen the powers of the President of the Commission.

☆ Reduce the power of veto—more use of qualified majority voting. National vetoes will remain on taxation and security issues following objections by the UK and Sweden.

☆ Groups of member states who wish to do so will be able to launch new policies before other members do.

New talks will take place in 2004 to define precise powers of national governments and EU institutions.

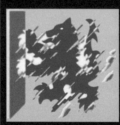

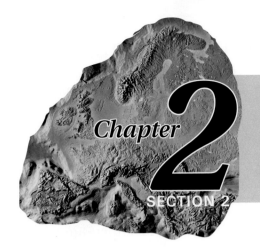

Chapter 2
SECTION 2

ECONOMIC ALLIANCES
BENEFITS OF EU MEMBERSHIP

What you will learn:

1 The reasons why countries have joined and why more want to join the EU:
- Trade Opportunities
- Access to EU Funds
- Agricultural Policy

A SINGLE EUROPEAN MARKET

The idea of creating a 'common market' dates back to the start of the European Union and the signing of the Treaty of Rome. The aim of the Single Market is to create an area within which goods, money, people and services can circulate freely without the restrictions of frontiers. The Single European Market was established in 1992.

Before then countries used to impose taxes and duties on imports. This was done to make their own goods cheaper and to encourage people to buy home-produced goods. Members of the European Union have agreed not to charge any of these tariffs on goods traded between member states. They have also agreed common levels of duty on certain goods entering the Union.

This agreement has increased competition within the European Union, meaning that people should get better value, choice and quality.

Citizens of all EU countries are now entitled to live and work in any other member state. In the past this was difficult because of different laws in the various countries. Now people have full entitlement to Social Security payments, benefits, medical care and education regardless of which European Union country they choose to live in. Efforts are being made to recognise educational qualifications in other countries. Your Standard Grade, Intermediate and Higher qualifications should be recognised and valued in France, Germany and so on.

HARMONISATION

Over 300 new laws have been passed as part of the completion of the Single European Market. These cover areas such as Trading Standards and Food Laws. Toys sold in the European Union should now carry the letters CE to show that they have met European safety standards. Food needs to list all the ingredients on the packaging. Even your school minibus has been affected by EU laws—it now has to have yellow warning plates at the front and back to show that it carries children and young people.

TRADE OPPORTUNITIES

Scottish businesses now have the chance to sell their products throughout the European Union. There are more than 350 million potential customers out there who might buy Scottish goods.

Of course, just as Scottish companies have the opportunity to expand into the European market, businesses in Germany, France and the other member states can now sell their goods in Scotland without any restriction. Highland Fountain Mineral Water would have to produce a very good product to compete with the well-known brands from continental Europe.

HIGHLAND FOUNTAIN
mineral water from Scotland

MEMO

From: Managing Director

To: Sales Director

As Britain is now part of the Single European Market, I suggest that we expand our sales force and employ new salespeople and representatives in the following European locations:

Frankfurt	Athens
Lyon	Vienna
Florence	Stockholm
Madrid	Antwerp

Our market research shows that there is demand for Scottish mineral water throughout Europe. It is up to us to fill the gap in the market and increase our sales.

ACTIVITIES

1 What is meant by a 'common market'?

2 How could the Single European Market be of direct benefit to you?

3 What is meant by harmonisation?

4 In what way can Highland Fountain Mineral Water benefit from the Single European Market?

5 What dangers must the company face up to as a result of the Single European Market?

THE COMMON AGRICULTURAL POLICY

The Common Agricultural Policy has been the cause of a great deal of controversy in Britain. Many politicians, and indeed ordinary people, in this country see the Common Agricultural Policy (CAP) as one of the major problems of the European Union. It takes up more than half of the entire budget of the EU and often leads to bitter disputes between member countries.

However, Britain's situation is different from most other European Union member countries. Only a very small proportion of our workforce is employed in agriculture. Although farming is very important in some areas of Britain, farmers themselves are not a large and powerful group in the country. The same is not true in France, for example, where agriculture employs a comparatively large proportion of workers and farmers are a very powerful and influential pressure group.

The Common Agricultural Policy has a number of aims. These include:
● ensuring a reasonable level of income for the farming community;

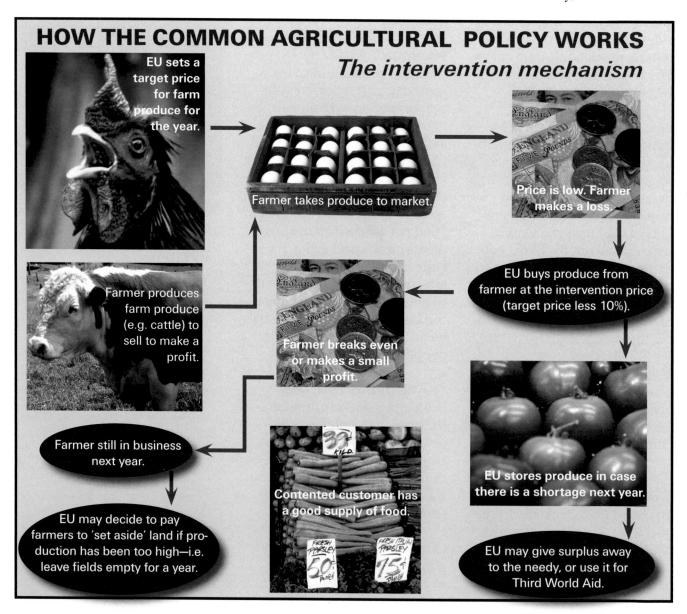

HOW THE COMMON AGRICULTURAL POLICY WORKS
The intervention mechanism

EU sets a target price for farm produce for the year.

Farmer takes produce to market.

Price is low. Farmer makes a loss.

Farmer produces farm produce (e.g. cattle) to sell to make a profit.

Farmer breaks even or makes a small profit.

EU buys produce from farmer at the intervention price (target price less 10%).

Farmer still in business next year.

Contented customer has a good supply of food.

EU stores produce in case there is a shortage next year.

EU may decide to pay farmers to 'set aside' land if production has been too high—i.e. leave fields empty for a year.

EU may give surplus away to the needy, or use it for Third World Aid.

- bringing agricultural prices together at the same level across the EU;

- preventing any one member state gaining an advantage in production due to cheap labour costs;

- ensuring steady supplies of all main food products, and therefore making sure that prices remain stable;

- improving the productivity of farms through modern technology and methods.

Benefits of the CAP

Ordinary people in the United Kingdom have benefited from the CAP in a number of ways. Food prices are relatively stable and there are seldom shortages of the main food products. Also, there is a wider choice of products from other EU countries.

The farming community has also benefited from the CAP. Firstly, it has given farmers guaranteed prices for products which means a more stable income for them. Secondly, the CAP has provided grants and subsidies to improve equipment and production methods on farms.

The CAP claims to guarantee reliable supplies of a wide range of products.

The CAP also produces surplus food which is often destroyed.

Criticisms of the CAP

Despite these benefits, people have criticised the CAP for leading to 'overproduction'. The EU is responsible for large 'food mountains' of surplus products such as butter, beef and grain. These surpluses are the result of guaranteeing prices to farmers. However, from time to time less well off people throughout the EU benefit from free handouts of surplus beef and butter which would otherwise need to be stored or destroyed.

If plans to expand the European Union go ahead, they could have a profound effect on the Common Agricultural Policy. Many of the countries that want to join are from Eastern Europe. For most of the second half of the twentieth century these were Communist countries and farming was controlled by the government. The change to private ownership has been difficult and farming methods remain inefficient and outdated. The Common Agricultural Policy would require substantial reform to cope with the entry of these countries to the Union.

ACTIVITIES

1. Why do some people feel that the Common Agricultural Policy is one of the biggest problems of the EU?

2. Why do people in France tend to feel differently about the CAP compared to people in Britain?

3. What are the aims of the CAP?

4. *"Ordinary people in Scotland have no reason to be happy with the CAP."*

   What evidence is there to suggest that this statement is biased or exaggerated?

5. Why are farmers usually happy with the way the CAP works?

6. Why are shop customers also usually happy with the way the CAP works?

7. Why will the inclusion of poorer ex-communist countries in the EU make it necessary to change the CAP?

AID TO THE REGIONS

Scotland benefits from the fact that the European Union distributes money to the comparatively poor regions of Europe. Studies are carried out to establish which areas in every EU country have lower than average incomes. Once these areas have been identified they are targeted for special help.

The money handed out by the EU is known as the Structural Fund. In fact, there are four different structural funds. (See below.)

The European Union does not give direct financial help to businesses. Instead, it will co-fund projects along with the Scottish Executive and local councils to improve the conditions in an area, making it more attractive for businesses to set up there. The theory is that if businesses can be attracted into a depressed area they will create jobs, raise income levels and contribute to a higher standard of living throughout the area.

When an application is made for funds it is usually the local council that prepares the submission. It must make sure that its plans match up with one of the three objectives and will lead to improved living standards. The EU may provide up to 50% of the cost for certain projects.

FACTFILE: Aid to the regions

OBJECTIVE STATUS

The European Union has three categories of assistance, called objectives.
Objective 1 includes areas where average incomes are less than 75% of the average for the whole EU. Almost 20% of the EU's population live in these areas.
Objective 2 includes areas that have seen a decrease in major employers, declining rural areas and areas dependent on fisheries. Approximately 18% of the EU's population live in such areas.
Objective 3 includes areas of long-term unemployment and places which have a particular difficulty with youth unemployment.

COMMUNITY INITIATIVES

There are four Community Initiatives:

INTERREG aims to stimulate cross-border, transnational and interregional cooperation.

LEADER promotes rural development through the initiatives of local action groups.

EQUAL provides for the development of new ways of combating all forms of discrimination and inequality as regards access to jobs.

URBAN encourages the economic and social regeneration of towns, cities and suburbs in crisis.

PRINCIPLES FOR AID

European Union aid to the regions is based on three principles.
Partnership
There must be involvement from national governments and local councils as well as from the EU.
Subsidiarity
The EU believes that decisions should be made at local level to ensure that the best use is made of available funds.
Additionality
EU money must be used in addition to rather than instead of money from within the country concerned.

EUROPEAN REGIONAL DEVELOPMENT FUND (ERDF)
Aims to reduce inequalities between the different regions of Europe.

EUROPEAN SOCIAL FUND (ESF)
Pays for training, vocational training and job creation measures.

EUROPEAN AGRICULTURAL GUARANTEE AND GUIDANCE FUND (EAGGF)
Pays for assistance to farmers, farming communities and rural areas.

COHESION FUND
Pays for projects related to the environment and transport infrastructure.

EU STRUCTURAL FUNDS

EXAMPLES OF PROJECTS FUNDED WITH EU ASSISTANCE (2001–02)

Project: Rosyth Zeebrugge Ferry Marketing Initiative

EU Funding: £700,000 which contributed to the costs of marketing the new direct vehicle ferry link between Rosyth and Zeebrugge.

Benefits: The new ferry will generate business. Scottish companies will find it easier to export goods. More tourists will visit Scotland. The environment will be improved because goods vehicles will not have to travel to English ports.

Project: Cairngorm Funicular Railway

Funding: £2.7 million

Benefits:
A new funicular railway to the summit of Cairngorm in the Central Highlands. The railway provides employment for local people. It will also be a major tourist attraction bringing people from Scotland and abroad into the area.

Project: Big in Falkirk
EU Funding: £190,000
Benefits: A festival of music and arts in Falkirk. The festival brought many visitors to the area. It also generated business for local companies.

Project:
Ettrick Mill Business Centre, Selkirk
EU Funding: £1.1 million
Benefits:
Support for new businesses in an area hit by unemployment. This will create jobs and stimulate the economy of a depressed area.

Burghead Promontary Initiative

Welcome to Burghead

EU Funding: £57,000

Benefits: Tourist-related developments at Burghead involving a nineteenth century storm signal and an Iron Age Fort. These will attract tourists to the area and provide employment for local people.

Project: Ardler Community Regeneration, Dundee

EU Funding: £933,936

Benefits: Projects to help a community affected by unemployment and other social problems. Ardler is a depressed area. This project aims to improve training opportunities and support for families. People will then be better equipped to look for jobs.

Project: Dumyat Business Park, Alloa
EU Funding: £319,000
Benefits: A development of Business Units in a depressed area. This area has been hit by the decline of traditional industries. The Business Park provides relatively cheap units for new businesses to use.

Project:
Pitlochry Railway Station Environmental Enhancement

EU Funding: £81,000

Benefits:
Improvement of the environment at Pitlochry Railway Station. Pitlochry is an important tourist town. The improvements to the railway station make the area more attractive to visitors and should increase trade for local businesses, creating jobs.

Case Study – EU Urban Funding

Source 1

Northern Glasgow

GLASGOW

URBAN Funding has been awarded to part of the Northern area of Glasgow, including Ruchill, Possil and the Royston Corridor (Royston, Provanmill and Blackhill). The area became heavily industrialised from the late nineteenth century. Heavy industries were attracted by the Forth and Clyde Canal and the newly built railways into the centre of Glasgow. In the latter part of the twentieth century the area suffered rapid industrial decline with high levels of unemployment and social deprivation. The public agencies in the city—Glasgow City Council, Scottish Homes, Glasgow Development Agency and Greater Glasgow Health Board came together to form the Glasgow Regeneration Partnership to apply for EU funding under the URBAN initiative. This is a strong partnership which will help the project to succeed.

Glasgow already receives some funding under the EU's Objective 2 programme, but the URBAN money will be focused on one of the most deprived areas. Most of the money will be spent on creating jobs and improving the environment.

Source 2

COMMUNITY CONCERNS

The following concerns were identified in consultation with members of the local community.

- Employment

- Housing

- Health

- Education and training

- Environment

- Culture

- Crime detection and prevention

- Sports and recreation

Source 3

"The Glasgow Northern Area is ideal for an URBAN programme. It meets the EU's criteria. The Glasgow Regeneration Partnership has put together an excellent proposal. It has set clear targets for what it hopes to achieve through EU funding. If these are met then there will be a very real and immediate improvement to the everyday lives of people in the area. Jobs will be created and people will have access to a wider range of training places."

View of EU spokesperson

"Why should all this funding be focused on the northern part of the city? The south side of the River Clyde also has major problems. I come from Govan and I believe that the problems there are just as bad as in Possil or Blackhill. And what about Pollok, Rutherglen, the Gorbals and so on? The money should be spread around to benefit all the people of Glasgow rather than just one small part of the city. Furthermore, this partnership is doomed to failure. Any organisation with so many different agencies involved is bound to run into problems. They will never agree on anything! Just wait and see!"

View of Bill Taylor

TRADE AND THE EUROPEAN UNION

THE COTONOU AGREEMENT

In April 2000 the EU signed a trade and aid agreement with almost eighty nations in Africa, the Caribbean and the Pacific (ACP). The historic agreement was reached in Cotonou, the capital city of the Republic of Benin. The Cotonou Agreement replaces the Lomé Convention which had organised links between the EU and the developing world for over twenty five years.

The new deal requires ACP countries enjoying special trade status with the European Union to respect human rights and democratic principles. The EU will provide 20 billion Euros worth of aid over seven years to the ACP countries provided they uphold

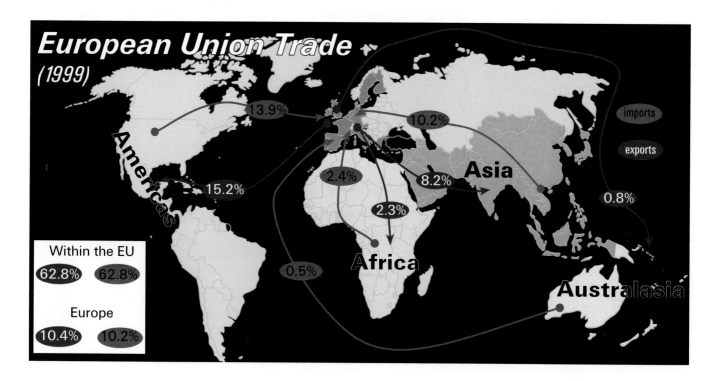

European Union Trade (1999)

13.9%
10.2%
imports
exports
15.2%
2.4%
8.2%
Asia
0.8%
2.3%
0.5%
Africa
Australasia
Americas

Within the EU
62.8%   62.8%
Europe
10.4%   10.2%

basic democratic principles. The new agreement also provides for a removal of restrictive trade barriers over the next fifteen years.

It is important for the EU to have good trade relations with ACP countries. Many of the products from these countries, including foodstuffs and minerals, cannot be produced within the EU. The Cotonou Agreement makes the EU a stronger economic force and allows it to buy these products at a cheaper price.

TRADE WARS WITH THE USA

As the EU has grown stronger and has acted in a united way, it has frequently come into economic conflict with the United States of America. The UK used to have very strong economic links with the USA but in recent years these have weakened as the UK has become closer to Europe.

The ideology of the USA is based on the principle of the free market. However, this includes the right to put up trade barriers if that is seen as being in the best interests of the USA. America has a long history of protecting its own trade and economic interests.

For years Europe and America locked horns over American tariffs on bananas from former French and UK colonies in the Caribbean, after US banana exporters' campaign contributions to the Clinton White House persuaded the administration to push the issue.

A row also broke out over growth hormones in beef. Brussels said it should be allowed to ban these on health grounds, leading to a European ban on American beef. This in turn led to trade barriers being imposed by America on certain European products.

In March 2002 the American President George Bush announced plans to impose tariffs of up to 30% on imported steel. He did this to protect the American steel industry from outside competition. Such a decision goes against the idea of free trade and the EU made immediate plans to retaliate by imposing 'smart levies' on goods that the USA exports to Europe. These would target products from industries that were politically important to President Bush. This row is only the latest in a series of transatlantic trade tussles.

ACTIVITIES

1   What is the Cotonou Agreement?

2   What conditions must ACP countries meet before the EU will trade with them?

3   Why is it important for the EU to have trade links with ACP countries?

4   Why have the UK's links with the USA weakened?

5   *"The USA and the EU have frequently fallen-out over trade issues. This is all the fault of the EU countries."*
      View of a journalist

   Give reasons to support and reasons to oppose the statement above.

6   Study Figure 2.2 showing the European Union's trade partners. What conclusions can be reached about the importance of trade with various parts of the world?

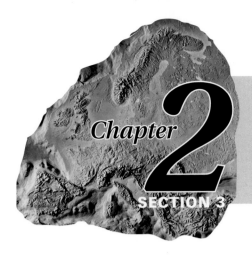

What you will learn:

1 The possible future enlargement of the EU.

2 The introduction of the Euro and the arguments for and against it.

CONDITIONS FOR EU MEMEBRSHIP

Any country which wants to join the European Union must satisfy a number of conditions. These were drawn up by the European Commission and are known as the Copenhagen Criteria. Each candidate country must have:

- a stable and democratic government
- a market economy which can compete with other EU countries
- a willingness to meet the aims of the EU
- a commitment to adopt EU laws

ENLARGEMENT OF THE EU

Austria, Finland and Sweden joined the European Union in 1995 bringing the total membership to fifteen. The Norwegian government was also keen for Norway to join but the people voted against the move in a referendum.

WIDENING V DEEPENING

At present there is a debate within the EU over whether its role should be widened or deepened. Widening means admitting more members; deepening means increasing the powers of the EU within the existing membership.

Members of the European Union

Applicants to the European Union

ENLARGING THE EU

It seems certain that the EU will be further enlarged during the first fifteen years of the twenty first century. Twelve countries have started negotiations to join the EU with Turkey also interested but unable to start discussions yet due to its political situation. When the Nice Treaty was signed in 2000, the existing member countries started to make plans for the enlargement of the Union—a process which will have profound implications for them.

At the Copenhagen Summit in December 2002 it was agreed that ten countries would join the EU from 2004. The addition of the Czech Republic, Slovakia, Slovenia, Estonia, Latvia, Lithuania, Poland, Hungary, Malta and Cyprus will add 75 million people to the EU. Romania and Bulgaria are also keen to join but will be unable to do so until 2007 at the earliest.

There are arguments for and against enlarging the European Union. These must be seen from the perspective of both the existing members and the applicant countries.

Advantages and Disadvantages of ENLARGEMENT

Advantages of Enlargement for Existing Members

✔ It opens up new markets for businesses. There would be a large demand for good quality products from countries such as Britain.

✔ It would create a more stable and peaceful Europe based on cooperation.

✔ Travel and trade would become easier over a wider area.

Advantages of Joining EU for Applicants

✔ They would have access to EU assistance from the Regional Development Fund.

✔ Support could be given to agriculture through the Common Agricultural Policy.

✔ New markets would open up for goods produced in applicant countries, with no barriers to trade with the rest of Europe.

✔ It would be a popular move with the people, therefore governments would gain popularity as well.

Disadvantages of Enlargement for Existing Members

✘ Regional Development Funds will be channelled towards poorer members.

✘ Common Agricultural Policy will be unable to cope with large rural economies such as that of Poland.

✘ Cheap labour will flood into existing member countries causing unemployment.

✘ Low wages in new member countries would encourage businesses to move there.

Disadvantages of joining EU for Applicants

✘ People from richer countries may buy up land and property in poorer countries.

✘ Some see that a loss of national identity could be a problem.

THE EUROSCEPTICS

Some people in Britain want the country to leave the European Union. This issue has caused disagreements within the Conservative Party which is split over its attitude towards Europe. People opposed to Britain's membership of the European Union are called Eurosceptics. They put forward several arguments to back their view.

Loss of Sovereignty
Britain has to give up power to the European Union, and fewer decisions are made at Westminster than before. Some people resent giving power to Brussels.

Britain's 'Special Relationship' with America
Britain has long-established links with the USA and these would be weakened if we integrated more with Europe. Britain also has traditional links with the Commonwealth countries such as Australia, Canada and New Zealand.

Cost
Britain's contributions to the EU budget are considerable. Some people believe that we do not get as much back as other countries because we are not a major agricultural nation.

The introduction of the Euro across most member countries

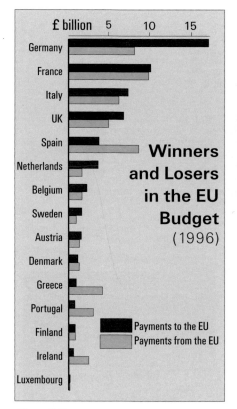

Winners and Losers in the EU Budget (1996)

£ billion: 5, 10, 15

Germany
France
Italy
UK
Spain
Netherlands
Belgium
Sweden
Austria
Denmark
Greece
Portugal
Finland
Ireland
Luxembourg

■ Payments to the EU
▧ Payments from the EU

Figure 2.3

in 2002 caused a further polarisation of views in the UK. However, it now seems unlikely that the UK could ever withdraw from the European Union. Politicians who argue for this viewpoint tend to be on the margins of mainstream politics. Most politicians now accept that the EU is here to stay and that the UK will play a major role in its development.

ACTIVITIES

1 What are the Copenhagen Criteria and why were they drawn up?

2 Explain the difference between 'widening' and 'deepening'.

3 *"The EU should concentrate more on deepening than widening at present."*

Do you agree with this statement? Give reasons to support your answer.

4 Why do so many countries want to join the European Union? What would be the advantages of membership for them?

5 *"There are no significant advantages in allowing more countries to join the EU."*
    View of a right-wing French politician

Write down two reasons to explain why the French politician could be accused of being selective in the use of facts.

6 *"There are no real disadvantages in allowing more countries into the European Union."*
   View of Italian politician

Write down two reasons to explain why the Italian politician could be accused of being selective in the use of facts.

7 Which UK political party has the largest number of Eurosceptics?

8 Briefly summarise the main arguments used by the Eurosceptics.

9 Study Figure 2.3.

   What conclusions can be reached about the following:
   • the countries that make a 'loss' from membership
   • the countries that make a 'profit' from membership

10 Which countries have the most reason to be unhappy with the way the EU budget works?

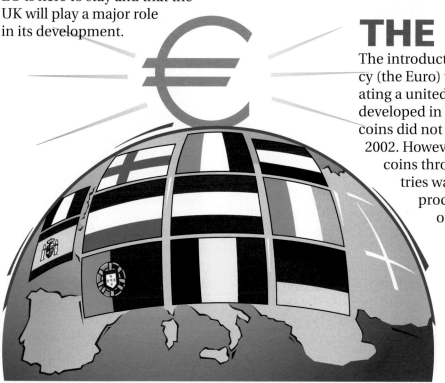

THE EURO

The introduction of a Single European Currency (the Euro) was the biggest step towards creating a united Europe. Plans for the Euro were developed in the 1990s but the new notes and coins did not come into being until 1 January 2002. However, the use of the same notes and coins throughout twelve European countries was only the superficial aspect of a process which linked the economies of the member nations.

SHOULD BRITAIN JOIN THE EURO?

Opinion in the UK is divided. The government has promised that it will hold a referendum on whether or not the UK should join the Euro. This could happen any time from 2003 onwards.

FINLAND

EIRE
NETHERLANDS
GERMANY
BELGIUM
LUXEMBOURG
FRANCE
AUSTRIA
ITALY
PORTUGAL
SPAIN
GREECE

EURO FINDING FAVOUR WITH SCOTS?

Tony Blair has said that there will be four months of 'campaigning' before a referendum is held. If the people vote 'yes' and decide to join the Euro, there would probably be a two-year delay before the new currency was introduced.

A referendum will not be held until the government is satisfied that the economy has passed five 'tests'. These were established by Gordon Brown, the Chancellor of the Exchequer, in 1997. They include whether joining a single currency would be good for jobs, for forcign investment and for the City; and whether the UK economy was in step with the economies of other European countries and if it had enough flexibility to adjust if this was not the case.

Which currency do you expect to be using within the next five years?

€ 60%

£ 32%

Don't know 8%

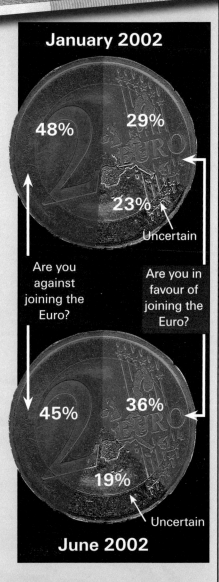

January 2002

48%   29%

23%
Uncertain

Are you against joining the Euro?

Are you in favour of joining the Euro?

45%   36%

19%
Uncertain

June 2002

Support for the Euro seems to be on the increase according to a July 2002 poll. Research by System Three, commissioned by the Scottish National Party, showed that more Scots were in favour of the Euro than six months previously. The survey was based on interviews with 972 adults across Scotland.

Scots were also asked which currency they expected to be using within the next five years. The results were surprising.

This poll suggested that Scots were less hostile to the Euro then people in other parts of the UK. A nationwide poll in June 2002 suggested that 58% of people were against joining the single currency with only 25% in favour.

What do people think of the EURO?

Brenda Howie, Finance Consultant

The Euro is forever—if it turns out to be a failure then we cannot leave. Why risk our economy when there are no real advantages?

Jim Clark, Teacher

The Euro would be really good for tourists and holidaymakers. When Real Madrid and Bayer Leverkusen played in the Champions League Final at Hampden many of their supporters were shocked to find that they could not use Euros in Scotland. It would also be better for us when we go on holiday. Instead of being charged commission on changing money from pounds to Euros, we could just use our own money in Spain, Portugal or Greece . . .

The issue of sovereignty has been exaggerated. France and Germany are part of the Euro but they have not lost their identity. British people are too inward-looking and defensive. We should take account of the benefits of being European rather than always thinking about the negative points . . .

A common currency will encourage foreign companies to invest in Britain. At the moment much of the investment from abroad is made on the assumption that we will join the Euro. If we do not, then much of that investment could be withdrawn, causing job losses and a downturn in the economy . . .

Billy Steele, Office Worker

Our economy is different from that of the rest of Europe. Far more people have mortgages with variable interest rates. In Europe most people either rent or have fixed interest rates. Joining the Euro would be damaging to the British economy.

We cannot afford to be left out in the cold. It is quite possible that every other member of the EU will be in the Euro. If we are not in it then we will be marginalised from the rest of Europe. We must look outwards . . ."

Andrea Kennedy, Shop Worker

We have already given up too much power to the EU. Britain is a proud and historic nation. We should retain our independence. Loss of sovereignty is a big issue and most people feel very strongly about it . . .

The British economy is strong—stronger than that of many of our European neighbours. If we join the Euro then our economy could be pulled down to the level of weaker economies. The events of 11 September 2001 were a case in point—the economy of the Euro-zone went into decline, but the British economy remained strong . . .

ITALIANS COMPLAIN ABOUT EURO INFLATION

In July 2002 Italian consumer groups called for a 'one day strike' from all shopping. The move was a protest against what they saw as unnecessary price rises following the introduction of the Euro earlier that year. When the new currency was introduced an exchange rate of 1 Euro to 2000 lire was set up. However, it seems that some businesses used an exchange rate of 1 Euro to 1000 lire, leading to price rises of 100%. The Italian government continues to insist that the switchover has gone smoothly and that it has been beneficial to Italians.

'The price rises have been much greater than anyone expected. When it comes to fruit and vegetables, prices are twice what I expect to pay when I convert back into old lire.

A Rome housewife

ACTIVITIES

1 Why was 1 January 2002 a key date for European integration?

2 What process will be used to decide whether or not Britain should join the Euro?

3 What economic conditions must be met before Britain joins the Euro?

4 Study the opinion poll results showing Scottish public opinion about the Euro and then answer the following question.

"Scottish people are clearly in favour of joining the Euro.
They believe that the Euro will soon be the currency that will be used in Scotland."

View of Tommy Walker

Give one reason to support and one reason to oppose the view of Tommy Walker.

5 Study 'What do people think about the Euro', then copy and complete a table like the one below. Try to identify which arguments are political, which are economic and which are cultural.

SUMMARY OF THE ARGUMENTS FOR AND AGAINST JOINING THE EURO		
	For	Against
Political		
Economic		
Cultural		

6 Why have some Italians complained about the introduction of the Euro?

7 Using all the information about the Euro, do you think that the UK should join the single currency? Give detailed reasons for your view.

8 You have been asked to carry out an investigation on the subject of the Euro.

  a) Write a hypothesis for your investigation. Explain why you think it is a good hypothesis.
  b) Give two detailed aims or headings that will help you to complete an investigation with the hypothesis you have chosen.
  c) You decide to carry out a survey like the one shown on page 46. What problems might you encounter when carrying out a survey of this type?

THE EUROPEAN UNION GLOSSARY OF TERMS

Amsterdam Treaty
The 1997 Amsterdam Treaty paved the way for the introduction of the Euro and for the enlargement of the EU.

Committee of the Regions
This EU body tries to form closer links between the EU and regional parliaments such as the Scottish Parliament.

Common Agricultural Policy
One of the main policies of the EU since it began although it will need big changes to cope with further enlargement.

Convergence criteria
The economies of member states had to pass various tests before joining the Euro.

Council of Europe
A body of more than forty countries that aims to protect human rights and promote democracy.

Council of the European Union
Main decision making body of the EU, made up of government ministers from all member states.

EMU
Economic and Monetary Union – the process of integrating the economies and currencies of the member states.

Enhanced cooperation
A process which allows keen countries to make faster progress towards integration than others.

Enlargement
The process of admitting new members to the European Union. By 2010 the EU could have as many as twenty seven members.

Euro
The Single European Currency, introduced in twelve member states from January 2002.

European Central Bank
Responsible for the Euro and for European monetary policy.

European Commission
Currently made up of twenty commissioners who are the driving force behind new legislation.

European Court of Human Rights
Linked to the Council of Europe, this court protects the basic rights of European people.

European Court of Justice
Monitors the application of European Law throughout the EU.

European Parliament
The directly-elected Parliament of the European Union. Critics say that its powers are limited.

Maastricht Treaty
This is the most important treaty in the history of the EU. It created the conditions for monetary union and the single currency amongst other things.

Nice Treaty (2000)
This sets out arrangements for enlarging membership of the EU by 2010.

Qualified majority voting
Most decisions in the EU are taken using this system, where larger countries have more say than smaller countries. However, larger countries on their own cannot force decisions through.

Rapid Reaction force
The EU intends to have its own Rapid Reaction Force of up to 60,000 troops. They could respond to developments within or outwith Europe.

Schengen Agreement
Since this agreement was signed in 1995 there have been no border controls between EU members on mainland Europe.

Single market
This guarantees the free movement of goods, people, services and money.

Treaty of Rome (1957)
This treaty set up the European Economic Community which has grown into the European Union.

Unanimity
Unanimous agreement is needed when the Council of the EU deals with controversial topics such as taxation, defence and social policy.

Veto
This helps countries to maintain national sovereignity in decision making. The power of veto lets one country stop a decision from being taken.

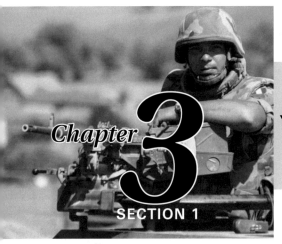

MILITARY ALLIANCES

YUGOSLAVIA

What you will learn:

1 The involvement of European nations with the UN and NATO.

2 What happened in the former Yugoslavia in the 1990s.

BACKGROUND TO THE CONFLICT

Yugoslavia was formed at the end of World War 1 as a confederation of different republics in the Western Balkans area. The country always experienced unrest and mistrust between the different nationalities who did not even share the same language, religion or culture. However, from the 1940s until the early 1980s the country was relatively stable. President Tito was a strong leader and although his socialist government was not always popular, Yugoslavia became the most prosperous and outward-looking country in Eastern Europe. Although a Communist himself, Tito always kept his distance from Moscow.

It was only when Tito died that the different groups in Yugoslavia became more noticeable and the country moved quickly towards break-up and civil war.

Countdown to disaster—THE BREAK-UP OF YUGOSLAVIA

1988—The province of Kosovo, where the population is split between Serbs and Albanians, witnesses rioting and disturbances. Serbs claim they have been victimised by the Albanians.

1989—Serb President Slobodan Milosevic takes over the semi-independent provinces of Kosovo and Vojvodina. This is seen as part of setting up a 'Greater Serbia'.

1990—Croatia and Slovenia threaten to leave Yugoslavia unless Serbia stops expanding.

1991—Croatia and Slovenia declare independence. Serbia sends in its army to try and bring them back into line. Serbia takes over substantial areas of Croatia.

1992—United Nations Protection Force (UNPROFOR) sends 14,000 troops to Croatia. Serbs

living in Croatia demand to be included in 'Greater Serbia'. War breaks out in Bosnia. Milosevic vows to protect Serbs from what he calls the 'Islamic fundamentalism of the Bosnian Muslims'. Three years of war follow between the Bosnian Muslims and the Bosnian Serbs, backed by the regular Serbian Army.

THE WAR IN BOSNIA

Bosnia is a small landlocked country, with Serbia to the east and Croatia to the west. Bosnia's capital is Sarajevo. The population is about 4.1 million. Before the war around 43% of the population were Bosnian Muslims, 32% were Serbs and 17% were Croats.

Each ethnic group had its own areas where it dominated the population. Other parts of Bosnia had a mixture of nationalities. Early in 1992 the Muslims and Croats voted for independence from Yugoslavia but the Bosnian Serbs were against any such move. They wanted to be integrated into the 'Greater Serbia' then being set up by Slobodan Milosevic.

The war in Bosnia lasted from 1992 until 1995. Atrocities were committed by all sides, including the massacre of up to 8,000 Muslims in Srebrenica by the Bosnian Serbs. They used a policy of 'ethnic cleansing' to drive Muslims out of Serb-held areas. Villages were torched and people were tortured and murdered as the situation got out of hand.

BOSNIA - HERZEGOVINA

Bihac · Banja Luka · Tuzla · Zenica · Srebrenica · Sarajevo · Mostar · Dubrovnik

THE ROLE OF THE UNITED NATIONS

From October 1992 United Nations forces were sent to Bosnia to protect aid convoys. Vital supplies of food and medicines were being stopped by the Serbs who had tightened their grip around Sarajevo. UN troops were given orders to protect the convoys but not to become involved in the fighting.

Negotiations
The European Union and the United Nations set up a joint negotiating team to try and bring the different groups around the conference table. They put forward a peace plan, known as the Vance-Owen Plan, which proposed dividing Bosnia into ten semi-independent provinces—three each for the Serbs, Croats and Bosnian Muslims, with one mixed province. The Bosnian Serb Parliament refused to accept the plan and it was scrapped.

Sanctions
The UN imposed trade and diplomatic sanctions on Serbia in protest at its military involvement in Bosnia. The Yugoslavian football team was banned from the 1992 European Championships—Denmark took its place and won the tournament!

Early in 1993 the UN declared the towns of Sarajevo, Srebrenica, Bihac and Gorazde to be 'Safe Areas'. They had previously been under constant bombardment by Serb artillery and air forces. However, the Serbs continued their attacks on Sarajevo and seemed poised to capture the city until NATO issued an ultimatum for them to withdraw or face air attacks.

Military threat
The diplomatic methods used by the UN to try and find a solution to the Bosnian conflict appeared to have failed. The growing involvement of NATO suggested that military methods were being considered. When a Serbian shell landed in a marketplace in Sarajevo, killing sixty civilians, NATO again threatened action and this time the Serbs did withdraw from their forward positions.

In 1995 Croatia launched a counter-attack and reclaimed areas lost to Serbia. At the same time NATO started three weeks of bombing of Serbian targets. This forced the Serbs to negotiate on the future of Bosnia, and in December 1995 all parties signed the Dayton Agreement to end the Bosnian War. A NATO-led peacekeeping force called I-FOR was sent to Bosnia to ensure that the Dayton Agreement was observed.

NATO's military power was required to enforce UN decisions in the Balkans.

More than 300 ethnic Kosovar Albanians, who have fled from the town of Junik in Kosovo, carry their belongings as they make their way through the Padosh valley when they arrive in the Albanian Padosh region after crossing the Kosovo-Albanian border. The refugees were forced out of Junik after Serbian police and troops started shelling the town.

WAR IN KOSOVO

Milosevic faced protests against his leadership and government throughout 1996 and 1997. He rode them out and looked for a way to win back the support of the Serbian people. He decided to make a stand over the province of Kosovo, on the southern edge of Serbia.

Kosovo was an area of great historic importance to the Serbs. However, by the 1990s the population of Kosovo was dominated by ethnic Albanians with the Serbs in a small minority. Milosevic had clamped down on the rights of the Albanians in Kosovo from the late 1980s onwards. The Albanian people formed the Kosovo Liberation Army (KLA) and conducted a guerilla war against what they saw as their Serb oppressors.

During the summer of 1997 KLA attacks on Serb police officers and officials intensified. In 1998

FACTFILE: NATO in Kosovo

* The total cost of the NATO bombing campaign was almost £5,000 million

* NATO started the raids because of ethnic cleansing by Serb forces in Kosovo

* 38,000 combat missions were carried out

* 344 allied aircraft were used

* 23,000 bombs and missiles were launched at Serbian targets

* 20% of these were precision-guided bombs or missiles

* More than 6,000 tonnes of explosives were dropped on Serbian targets

* No NATO forces were killed in the operations

* Approximately 500 civilians died as a result of the raids

* As a result of the raids Serbia agreed to withdraw from Kosovo

the Serbian government sent troops into Kosovo, supposedly to deal with the KLA, but killing many innocent civilians as well. Throughout 1998 and the early months of 1999 Serb forces attacked Kosovar targets and started a policy of ethnic cleansing. Ethnic Albanians were driven from their homes and became refugees. The UN and NATO attempted to broker peace settlements but by March 1999 it was clear that they were not working.

During March 1999 NATO began a campaign of air strikes against Serbia, effectively declaring war on Milosevic's government. The strikes lasted for seventy eight days and were not confined to Kosovo, but included attacks on targets throughout Serbia. Many Serbian civilians were killed or injured and key industrial and transport targets were destroyed.

By June 1999 the Milosevic government, in the face of serious damage, was forced to negotiate a peace deal. Serb forces were withdrawn from Kosovo to be replaced by a peacekeeping force known as the Kosovo Force (KFOR).

KFOR

KFOR was a NATO-led international force responsible for establishing and maintaining security in Kosovo following the Serb withdrawal. KFOR entered Kosovo on 12 June 1999 under a United Nations mandate, two days after the adoption of UN Security Council Resolution 1244.

KFOR was faced with a huge challenge. Kosovo was facing a grave humanitarian crisis. Military and paramilitary forces from the Federal Republic of Yugoslavia (FRY) and the Kosovo Liberation Army (KLA) had been fighting for months. Ethnic tensions were high and had claimed the lives of many civilians. Almost one million people had fled Kosovo to seek refuge where their lives would not be endangered.

The objectives of KFOR were:
- to establish and maintain a secure environment in Kosovo, including public safety and order;
- to monitor, verify and, when necessary, enforce compliance with the agreements that ended the conflict;
- to provide assistance to the UN Mission in Kosovo (UNMIK).

KFOR was made up of 50,000 troops. Nearly 40,000 troops were deployed in Kosovo and another 7,500 provided support from neighbouring countries such as Macedonia. Russian troops were involved in supporting KFOR. Some 850,000 Albanians who had been driven out of Kosovo returned, while 200,000 Serbians fled, fearful of what might happen to them under Albanian control.

British RAF Harrier Jump Jets were deployed in the air strikes against Serbia

ACTIVITIES

1 *"The death of Tito was the event which plunged Yugoslavia into chaos."*
   Give evidence to support this statement.

2 Which component part of the former Yugoslavia seemed to be guilty of trying to expand into other areas?

3 *"Bosnia has a mixed population."*
   Give evidence to support this statement.

4 What is meant by 'ethnic cleansing'?

5 Describe the role of the UN in the former Yugoslavia.

6 Describe the role of NATO during the Kosovo conflict.

7 Do you believe that the NATO air strikes on Serbia were justified? Use information from the factfile to support your answer.

8 Describe the composition of KFOR.

WAR CRIMES

Slobodan Milosevic appeared for the fourth time before the court of the International Criminal Tribunal for the former Yugoslavia in The Hague, on 11 December 2001.

The charges against him related to:

⚖ atrocities carried out in Kosovo in 1999

⚖ crimes against humanity committed in Croatia between 1991 and 1992

⚖ alleged genocide in Bosnia-Herzegovina between 1992 and 1995.

Since 1999 efforts have been made to bring to justice some of the war criminals from the Yugoslavian conflict. The incidents investigated range from small-scale local events right up to the indictment of Yugoslav President Milosevic for war crimes.

Milosevic lost the 2000 Presidential election to Vojuslav Kostunica in Yugoslavia but attempted to 'fiddle' the results. The people turned against him and he was removed from office. In the early hours of 1 April 2001 Milosevic was arrested after heavily armed police laid siege to his Belgrade house for 36 hours. He was taken to The Hague to face trial in front of the UN International Tribunal for War Crimes.

The indictment relating to Bosnia—the most serious—accused him of being responsible for the killing of thousands of Bosnian Muslims and Bosnian Croats. It specifically mentioned the 1995 massacre at Srebrenica and accused Mr Milosevic of involvement in the murder, imprisonment and mistreatment of thousands of civilians, including women and the elderly.

In total around 100 suspects were indicted by the Hague Tri-

Forensic experts examine a mass grave in Kamenica, Bosnia, 25 July 2002, near the site of the notorious 1995 Srebrenica massacre. The remains of fifteen people had already been found in the grave, believed to contain 100 bodies. More than 7,000 Bosnian Muslims were killed by Serb forces after the fall of Srebrenica, in Europe's worst massacre since World War II.

bunal. Some were still at large in 2003. Of those, the most prominent were the Bosnian Serb leaders Radovan Karadzic and Ratko Mladic, indicted for atrocities during the 1992–95 Bosnian war. The Bosnian-Serb Prime Minister Mladan Ivanic said he would do "everything possible" to ensure they are handed over.

Four Serb leaders, besides Mr Milosevic, were wanted for alleged war crimes in Kosovo: Serbian President Milan Milutinovic, former Yugoslav Deputy Prime Minister Nikola Sainovic, the Yugoslav army's former chief-of-staff General Dragoljub Ojdanic, and former Serbian

Minister of the Interior Vlajko Stojiljkovic.

Three former Yugoslav army officers—Mile Mrksic, Miroslav Radic and Veselin Sljivancanin—were indicted for the 1991 massacre of at least 200 ethnic Croats in the eastern Croatian city of Vukovar.

WITNESS statements

Djakovica

Refugees in Albania reported that Yugoslav army units shelled the streets of Djakovica while paramilitary police armed with knives moved through different neighbourhoods expelling families. Witnesses said that between 100 and 200 men were rounded up and shot. These killings were separate from apparently random shootings in the street. There were allegations of rape with young women and girls repeatedly abused by Serb paramilitary soldiers.

It is believed that Serb units killed between 200 and 300 men as they systematically cleared villages around Djakovica on a single day in April 1999. Survivors say Serb forces separated men aged between 18 and 65 from their families and shot them by the roadside. Many of the men were forcibly taken from convoys of refugees heading for the border. Later, a BBC reporter visited one field and filmed evidence of the remains of at least 100 men, their bodies decomposing where they had fallen.

Bela Cerkva

Nesim Popaj, the village doctor, was shot in front of his wife and children by a police commander who called him a "terrorist".

The Serb commander then put his boot on the head or neck of Mr Popaj's 18-year-old nephew Shendet, before shooting the teenager dead. Some of the villagers were ordered to strip naked and forced to hand over valuables.

"They started shooting with automatic guns," Zenel Popaj, brother of Nesim, told Panorama. "People fell on top of me I stayed very still for 15 minutes." Mr Popaj and a two-year-old boy, believed to have been shielded by his mother, were the only survivors. Seven women and three children were amongst a total of over fifty dead.

The Serb forces moved on and shot at least seven elderly villagers in a nearby field. Overall, fifty four members of a village with a population of only a few hundred were killed.

Summary of the role of the *UN* and *NATO* in the former Yugoslavia

Role of the UN	Role of NATO
● Peacekeeping	● Policing a no-fly zone to prevent air attacks on Bosnia
● UNHCR (UN High Commission for Refugees) involved	● Air strikes against Serbian military targets in and around Bosnia
● Investigating war crimes and setting up the International Tribunal on War Crimes in the Former Yugoslavia	● Sending a Multi-National Force to enforce the Dayton Peace Agreement in Bosnia
	● Air strikes against Serbia during the Kosovo crisis
	● Providing troops for KFOR to take control of Kosovo after the Serbian withdrawal

ACTIVITIES

1 What happened to Slobodan Milosevic after the Kosovo war?

2 Study the witness statements about war crimes in Kosovo. What conclusions can be reached about the following:

  • The behaviour of Serb forces in Kosovo?
  • The numbers of people killed?

3 Using the Summary of the Role of the UN and NATO in the former Yugoslavia, write a short essay comparing the extent to which each organisation was effective.

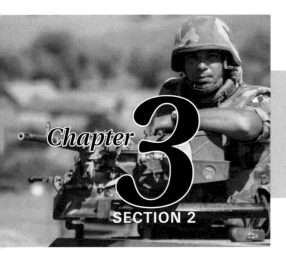

MILITARY ALLIANCES

THE NORTH ATLANTIC TREATY ORGANISATION

THE ORIGINS AND FORMATION OF NATO

During World War II Britain, the United States of America and the Soviet Union fought together against the common enemy of Nazi Germany. However, as the war went on, the relationship between the 'Allies' became more and more uneasy. In particular, Britain and America began to mistrust the Soviet Union.

By the end of the War the Soviet Union had freed most of Eastern and Central Europe from German control. The Allies argued over which of them should 'occupy' the liberated areas, and the uneasy relationship between them became a deep split. The Soviet Union went its own way. It had a different ideology and used its power to dominate Eastern Europe.

Britain, the United States, Canada and the liberated countries of Western Europe decided to join together to form the North Atlantic Treaty Organisation (NATO). NATO was established in April 1949. The main aim of the organisation was to protect Western Europe from any further expansion by the Soviet Union. Eastern Europe had come under Moscow's control and communist governments had been established in what were now known as the 'satellite states' of the USSR.

NATO aimed to keep the peace in Europe through a collective defence policy. The idea was that if any NATO member was attacked, this would be seen as an attack on the whole organisation.

After 1949 there was no further expansion of Communism and no major wars have been fought in Europe. Therefore it can be argued that NATO has been a success.

HOW NATO WORKS

NATO has been able to ensure that the military forces and defence policies of the member countries have been planned and organised in a cooperative way.

The member countries had the shared aim of trying to prevent any further expansion of Communism, and they put this into practice through military cooperation. The Western European countries might not have been able to put together such a strong military alliance on their own, therefore the presence of the United States was vital.

All NATO forces come under the command of Allied Command Europe (ACE) which was set

The Secretary General of NATO, Lord Robertson, is the head of the organisation. He was appointed by all of the member states.

up to defend Europe from the possible threat of Soviet invasion. The command structure remains basically the same although there is no current threat from Russia. NATO built up a huge store of conventional and nuclear weapons. It carried out regular military exercises and intensive training programmes to make sure that it would be ready if the attack ever came.

NATO's top decision making body is the Council, made up of politicians from all the member countries. Military planning and training is the responsibility of the Military Committee, formed by the Chief of Defence Staffs from each country. NATO's main offices are in Brussels, and the military headquarters, the Supreme Headquarters Allied Powers Europe (SHAPE), are nearby at Mons.

BACKGROUND TO THE COLD WAR

From 1945 until the late 1980s, the USA and the USSR opposed each other in what was known as the Cold War. They never took part in direct armed conflict with each other, but at times the world was close to a war between the two superpowers.

Why did the USA and the USSR hate each other so much? The answer lies in the different ideologies of each country.

The ideology in the United States of America was capitalism. The USA had a history of democracy and human rights, and under the capitalist economic system people had great individual freedom to live and work as they wanted to. Many people were able

to become rich and enjoy great personal wealth.

In the USSR the ideology was communism. Under this system the government controlled most aspects of people's lives. There was little individual freedom and no regular elections which could change the government. People were not allowed to leave the country without government approval.

Both countries were convinced that their ideology was the best one. Each was frightened that the other superpower would try and expand its influence over a wider area. Therefore, to try and prevent any spread of a hated ideology, the superpowers built up alliances to strengthen their positions.

NATO played a big part in the Cold War since it was the military alliance between the United States and the major Western European nations, who were concerned by the threat from Moscow.

WHY DID THE COLD WAR END?

Throughout the 1960s, '70s and early '80s attempts were made by the leaders of the USA and the USSR to reach agreements on Arms Control and to limit the development of new weapons. Despite some agreements the picture still looked bad in the early 1980s with developments such as Cruise Missiles, SS20s and the American Strategic Defence Initiative (Star Wars).

President Reagan, elected in 1980, seemed to be taking a very hard line in dealings with Moscow, and the Soviet leaders of the time were part of the old-fashioned Communist tradition.

EUROPE DURING THE COLD WAR

Europe was divided by the Iron Curtain after 1945. The USSR dominated Eastern Europe and NATO was formed in Western Europe along with Canada and the USA.

USA

CANADA

ICELAND
SWEDEN
FINLAND
NORWAY
IRELAND
UNITED KINGDOM
DENMARK
N
B
LUXEMBURG
WEST GERMANY
EAST GERMANY
POLAND
USSR
FRANCE
SWITZERLAND
AUSTRIA
CZECHOSLOVAKIA
HUNGARY
ROMANIA
ITALY
YUGOSLAVIA
Black Sea
BULGARIA
PORTUGAL
SPAIN
ALBANIA
GREECE
TURKEY

NATO MEMBERSHIP

Original Members (1949):

Belgium	Luxembourg
Canada	Netherlands
Denmark	Norway
France	Portugal
Iceland	United Kingdom
Italy	United States

Later members:

West Germany (1955)
Greece (1952)
Spain (1982)
Turkey (1952)

KEY
N=Netherlands
B=Belgium
Members of NATO
Iron Curtain

There seemed to be little hope of progress.

The influence of Gorbachev
This all changed when the Soviet Union chose Mikhail Gorbachev as its new leader in 1985. He represented a new generation of Communists and he was quick to seek change. In his own country he developed the policies of 'glasnost' and 'perestroika', making government more open and accountable and trying to modernise the economy.

Within a couple of years it was clear that Gorbachev was concerned mainly with trying to improve the situation within the USSR and was not really bothered about fighting a 'Cold War' with the outside world. Agreements were reached to reduce arms and destroy whole classes of weapons. The countries of Eastern Europe began to change. If any of them had shown defiance against Moscow in the 1950s and '60s, they would have been invaded; in the late 1980s Gorbachev actually encouraged them to change.

The fall of Communism
A series of revolutions swept across Eastern Europe as the Communists were removed from power and democratic elections were held. In Poland, Czechoslovakia, Bulgaria, Albania, Hungary and East Germany this happened relatively peacefully, but in Romania there was a period of fighting before the Communists were overthrown.

The ideological division which had split Europe was removed. Germany was reunited and the old links between East and West were re-established.

Gorbachev had hoped to keep the Soviet Union together as one country, and he had wanted to reform the economy and improve living standards. However, he was unable to do so. Various parts of the old Soviet Union broke away and became independent, including some of the nations of the 'New Europe'—

Lithuania, Estonia, Latvia, Belarus, Ukraine etc.

Opponents of Gorbachev criticised him for not making changes quickly enough and he was replaced as leader in Moscow by Boris Yeltsin. However, Gorbachev will always be remembered as the politician who was brave enough to bring the Cold War to an end and lay the foundations for a more peaceful Europe.

NATO'S CHANGING ROLE
NATO changed its goals and policies following the end of the Cold War. The main points of the new strategy included:
- Less dependence on nuclear weapons. NATO is less likely to be involved in a major superpower conflict than before.

(continued on page 60)

Secretary General of the UN , Kofi Annan, visiting NATO for discussions with the then Nato Secretary General, Dr. Javier Solana in 1999.

ACTIVITIES

1 When and why was NATO established?

2 Why is it accurate to describe NATO as 'The Atlantic Alliance'?

3 Why was the presence of the USA vital to NATO?

4 Briefly describe the ideologies of the USA and the USSR during the Cold War years.

5 What was 'The Cold War'?

DO WE STILL NEED NATO?

NATO was formed to challenge the threat which the USSR posed for countries in Western Europe. With the collapse of the USSR, many people see no point in NATO continuing to exist.

Throughout the 1960s, '70s and '80s NATO countries armed themselves with highly sophisticated, but extremely expensive, weapons systems. The phrase 'the peace dividend' is used to describe the opportunity which exists to save the huge amount of money that used to be spent on the development and manufacture of weapons.

ARGUMENTS FOR ENDING NATO

✘ NATO was established to stop the spread of Communism from the Soviet Union. Similar organisations were established in Central Asia (CENTO) and South-east Asia (SEATO). They have achieved their purpose and now have no role to play.

✘ The Cold War is over. The great ideological differences no longer exist. Europe is a united continent. The idea of a defence force based on ideology is out of date.

✘ European countries should have their own military alliance without relying on the USA. The USA 'defended' Europe simply to avoid fighting a war on its own soil. Europe should go its own way.

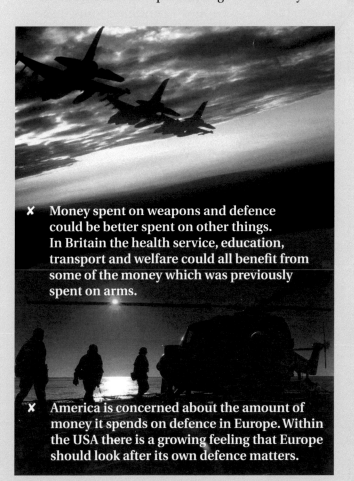

✘ Money spent on weapons and defence could be better spent on other things. In Britain the health service, education, transport and welfare could all benefit from some of the money which was previously spent on arms.

✘ America is concerned about the amount of money it spends on defence in Europe. Within the USA there is a growing feeling that Europe should look after its own defence matters.

ARGUMENTS FOR RETAINING NATO

✔ 11 September 2001 showed that there is a new threat to world peace from international terrorism. NATO is the body with the power and the organisation to combat Al Qaeda and other terrorist groups.

✔ The former Soviet Union could still become unstable. Extreme politicians, some of whom have Communist beliefs, could come to power. There is unrest and conflict in various areas of the former USSR including the Chechen Republic, Georgia and Armenia. NATO might still face a military threat from the former USSR.

✔ The former Yugoslavia remains an area of possible conflict. Montenegro, which in 2002 was part of what remained of Yugoslavia, could look for independence in line with other parts of the country. Macedonia is an unstable country with links to Albania and Kosovo. NATO could be needed to intervene in future Balkan conflicts.

✔ Maverick leaders such as Saddam Hussein (Iraq) and Colonel Gaddaffi (Libya) have been a threat to the developed world for many years now. If NATO remains as a united force then these leaders and others like them will be less able to exert an influence over world events.

✔ The consequences of dismantling NATO would be very expensive. The military industry creates thousands of jobs and boosts the economies of the areas involved. Reductions in American forces in Germany have already had a negative economic impact.

✔ NATO has kept the peace effectively for more than fifty years—why risk changing this?

- More flexible forces, able to undertake a variety of tasks. In the past, NATO forces had expected an attack from Russia and nowhere else.

- Greater use of multinational forces. Before, NATO was organised along the lines of cooperation between national armies; now forces are made up of troops from a number of different countries.

- Active involvement in international peacekeeping forces.

- More cooperation with other international organisations like the UN.

Partnership for Peace

The North Atlantic Cooperation Council was set up to bring NATO members closer to the countries of Eastern Europe and the former Soviet Union. Some of the former Communist countries would now like to join NATO itself.

In January 1994, NATO launched its Partnership for Peace policy, which set up a process by which the Eastern European countries will become closer to NATO, leading eventually to full membership.

Flexible response

During the Cold War the close links between the USA and Europe were vital in the defence against Communism. During the 1990s the ties were loosened and many American bases in the UK and Germany were closed. The American submarine base at the Holy Loch, near Dunoon, was one of those to close. The events of 11 September 2001 forced a rethink on the links between Europe and the USA. The USA realised that it needed close ties with its European allies in the war against terrorism. However, in this war there was no clear 'battleground' and the members of NATO needed to be prepared to make a flexible response to threats from all over the world.

NATO's role in the former Yugoslavia

NATO may have a role to play as a 'world policeman'. During the war in the former Yugoslavia in the 1990s NATO was used as 'muscle' to enforce UN resolutions and policies. When diplomacy and discussion failed, NATO was brought in to take military action. It was the involvement of NATO that led to the removal of Slobodan Milosevic from power and to the creation of peace in Bosnia and Kosovo. NATO action included enforcing a 'no-fly zone' around Bosnia and a campaign of bombing against Serbian industrial and military targets during the Kosovo conflict. (See pages 50–55.)

THE WESTERN EUROPEAN UNION

During recent modernisation of NATO the military forces of most member countries have been significantly reduced and reorganised. New tactics have been introduced to give them greater mobility and flexibility and to make it easier for forces from non-member countries to take part in NATO operations. One of the most important developments has been the concept of 'Combined Joint Task Forces' (CJTFs).

In 1994, NATO committed itself to supporting the development

NATO troops act as riot police in a peacekeeping role in the Balkans

of a much stronger European Security and Defence Identity or 'ESDI'. NATO is working with the Western European Union, (the WEU)—the EU security organisation—in order to achieve this.

Rapid Reaction Force

The EU has announced its intention to create a Rapid Reaction Task Force of some 60,000 troops to deal with security threats within Europe. This force would be able to undertake the full range of the so-called Petersberg tasks set out in the Amsterdam Treaty of 1997. These consist of:

- humanitarian and rescue tasks;
- peacekeeping tasks;
- tasks of combat forces in crisis management, including peacemaking.

Its role would be to undertake military operations led by the EU in response to international crises, in circumstances where NATO as a force was not involved. This process is part of the EU's plan to develop a common European policy on security and defence. Measures have been introduced which would enable the Western European Union to use NATO troops and equipment for WEU-led operations.

These arrangements are designed to avoid creating duplication of command and management of forces within Europe. They will allow the European members of NATO to take greater responsibility in European security affairs. Some see this as allowing Europe to run its own affairs; others interpret it as a signal that the USA does not want to take so much to do with Europe. Over time it is to be expected that the Western European Union will be increasingly associated with the structures of the European Union itself, leading to a clearer development of European Union policy on defence and security issues.

The scene is the House of Commons in London. The Speaker has just called Mrs Pauline McKenzie, Scottish Socialist MP for the constituency of Glenstirling, to ask a question.

Report from the Commons

Mrs McKenzie – I am very concerned about the fact that UK defence spending is still as high as it was in the past. The Cold War ended years ago. We no longer need the forces which were considered necessary then. Can the Minister explain why our defence spending is still so high?

Minister – Britain has a major role to play within NATO and must honour commitments made to other members. However, we have made cutbacks in the manpower of the armed services, with several regiments being disbanded in the coming year. We feel that this meets our defence needs in the changing world at present.

Mrs McKenzie – But that isn't the real problem, is it? The massive costs for our defence come from our nuclear submarine fleet and the Trident missiles which they carry. To make real savings on defence Britain would need to scrap its nuclear forces.

Minister – Britain has its own nuclear deterrent and that is how it should stay. Trident is one of the most sophisticated and accurate missile systems in the world. We are the envy of many other nations because we have Trident and they do not.

Mrs McKenzie – We do not need Trident missiles and nuclear submarines. Perhaps we should consider the advantages of a strong non-nuclear defence strategy. The threats to peace don't come from the major superpowers these days. Russia wants to join NATO, and China is our economic ally. The flashpoints today are in areas such as the Middle East and the Balkans. Don't tell me we would use nuclear weapons in these places. And anyway, the biggest threat is from international terrorism — our worst enemies may be in our own back yard! Britain's future defence role will be as part of an international peacekeeping force and a coalition against terrorism. We should keep our conventional forces as they are, instead of disbanding regiments. Conventional forces are much cheaper to operate and will be of more use in the future than hi-tech nuclear missile systems that could wipe out cities at the press of a button.

Minister – The government believes that we need a balanced defence policy to prepare for all possibilities. Our independent nuclear deterrent makes us safe from attack. There are many countries now with a nuclear capability — what if the likes of Iraq or Libya had nuclear weapons?

Mrs McKenzie – And what about the money that could be saved? That could then be spent on the Health Service, Education and other worthwhile projects. You lot should get your act together and stop making the world a more dangerous place.

Speaker – Order, Order.

THE FUTURE OF NATO

Partnership For Peace

In 1994, NATO launched the Partnership for Peace (PfP). The main objective of the Partnership was to improve the links between NATO members and Partner countries in Eastern Europe, most of whom wanted to join NATO at some point in the future. Twenty seven countries now participate. The Partnership for Peace is an example of how NATO has tried to improve security by cooperation with other countries.

ACTIVITIES _____

1   What is meant by 'The Peace Dividend'?

2   Study the arguments for and against retaining NATO.

    In your own opinion, should NATO continue?

    Give reasons to support your answer and explain why you have rejected the other view.

3   In what ways did NATO change its policies after the end of the Cold War?

4   How is America's attitude towards NATO changing?

5   What are CJTFs?

6   Describe the size and tasks of the EU's Rapid Reaction Task Force.

7   How will the links between the WEU and the EU develop?

    Compare the views of the government minister and Pauline McKenzie M.P. on page 61.

8   What are the main differences in their opinions about the amount the government should spend on defence?

9   Overall, which one of them do you agree with? Give reasons for your answer.

Relations With Russia

NATO regards Russia as vital to European security. It is the largest and most populated country in Europe. It also has access to nuclear weapons and other military hardware developed during the Cold War years. In 1996, NATO proposed to Russia that they should develop jointly a new cooperative relationship. The result of this was the NATO-Russia Founding Act, signed in May 1997, and the establishment of a NATO-Russia Permanent Joint Council (PJC).

The PJC provides the mechanism by which NATO and Russia can consult regularly on political and security-related issues, including peacekeeping, nuclear safety, defence conversion, arms control and environmental protection. It also provides the framework for military cooperation between NATO and Russia.

NATO knows that security in Europe cannot be built fully without Russia, and that it must try to improve trust and cooperation. The mutual suspicions which existed between East and West during the Cold War belong to the past, but there is always a possibility of political change in Russia. Hard-line Communists still exist in mainstream politics and NATO is aware that they must guard against any return to the ideologies of the Cold War.

Russia suspended cooperation with NATO following the beginning of the air campaign initiated by the Alliance in March 1999 to end the conflict in Kosovo. However, when the air campaign ended, Russia agreed to contribute significant forces to the NATO-led Kosovo Force (KFOR), set up under United Nations auspices to prevent a resumption of the conflict and to create the conditions for peace. NATO Secretary General Lord Robertson (a former Scottish MP) visited Moscow in February 2000. There was agreement to start a proper dialogue on a wide range of security issues in the future.

Recent Changes

NATO has worked very hard to develop positive relations with Russia with a view to promoting understanding and establishing cooperation on a permanent basis. NATO has also sought to develop relations with Ukraine. The ultimate aim is to bring these countries into NATO as new members.

NATO has tried to expand the role of European countries in its leadership. During the Cold War the USA was seen as the 'leader' of the Alliance. Since the end of the Cold War the American involvement has lessened. The USA is less directly affected by events in Europe that do not have a global significance. NATO has changed from being one of the two major global superpower blocs to being the single important military bloc in the European area. For many years the European member countries provided the major part of the military forces stationed in Europe, but much of the cost of transatlantic security, as well as the task of playing the lead role in the political development of the Alliance, was taken by the United States. Today the balance is gradually being readjusted. North America and Europe are playing more equal roles.

Operation Essential Harvest was a 30-day mission by NATO forces in 2000 to disarm Albanian rebels operating in Macedonia. This type of mission may be typical of the type of work NATO could undertake in future years.

Enlargement

Since its foundation in 1949, the Alliance has remained open to new member countries able to meet the obligations and responsibilities of membership. At the Madrid Summit Meeting in July 1997, the NATO Allies decided to invite three prospective new member countries to begin negotiations on joining: the Czech Republic, Hungary and Poland. The three countries formally became members of NATO in March 1999.

Expansion looks set to continue. NATO foreign ministers considered at least nine new applications for membership at a summit in Prague in November 2002. The possibility that the Baltic states—Estonia, Latvia and Lithuania—could be admitted rings loud alarm bells in Moscow.

Some experts predict that expansion will make an already unwieldy alliance even less effective and that, rather than spreading stability throughout Europe, it is simply leading to possible instability.

The new relationship with Russia is seen by many as proof that NATO has made the decision to transform its agenda from that of the Cold War into one where the focus is on combating major

international threats such as terrorism and the spread of weapons of mass destruction.

ACTIVITIES

1. What is the main objective of the Partnership for Peace?

2. Why is Russia so important to European security?

3. Why did Russia suspend cooperation with NATO in 1999?

4. In what way has the balance of power within NATO shifted?

5. Which three countries joined NATO in 1999?

6. What effect might further enlargement have on NATO?

7. What was Operation Essential Harvest?

8. From Table 3.1 what conclusions can be reached about the average strength of armed forces in NATO countries?

   You should reach conclusions about each of the following:

   - The countries with the largest armed forces in 1990 and 2001

   - The countries which have seen the smallest decrease in the strength of their armed forces since 1990

   - The countries which have seen the largest decrease in the strength of their armed forces since 1990

9. *"All NATO member countries have seen a decrease in defence spending per capita between 1990 and 2001."*

   Statement by journalist

   To what extent is the journalist guilty of selective use of facts?

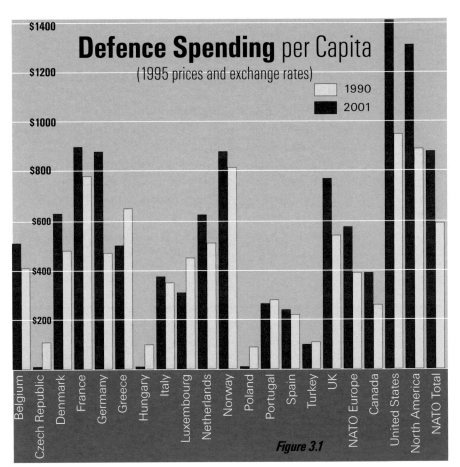

Defence Spending per Capita
(1995 prices and exchange rates)
☐ 1990
■ 2001

Figure 3.1

ARMED FORCES – annual average strength (000)

	1990	2001
Belgium	106	41
Czech Republic		49
Denmark	31	25
France	550	367
Germany	545	307
Greece	201	211
Hungary		49
Italy	493	347
Luxembourg	1	1
Netherlands	104	52
Norway	51	31
Poland		178
Portugal	87	70
Spain	263	134
Turkey	769	795
United Kingdom	308	219
Canada	87	59
United States	2,181	1,482
NATO Total	5,778	4,445

Table 3.1

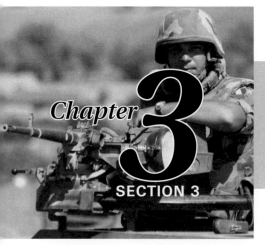

MILITARY ALLIANCES
THE UNITED NATIONS AND PEACEKEEPING

What you will learn:

1   The role of each of the main parts of the UN.

2   The methods used by the UN to try to maintain peace and security.

FACTFILE: The United Nations

The General Assembly

The General Assembly of the United Nations is the main forum for debate and discussion. All of the members—there were 191 in 2003—have a seat in the General Assembly and they have one vote each, no matter how large or small they are. The General Assembly decides on many issues to do with the United Nations, but peacekeeping and conflict are the responsibility of the Security Council.

The Security Council

The Security Council consists of fifteen members. Five of these are permanent members (China, France, Russia, the UK and the USA), and ten are non-permanent members. These change every two years, with five of them coming from Africa and Asia, one from Eastern Europe, two from Latin America and two from Western Europe and the rest of the world. Some members of the UN want the number of permanent members to be reduced.

THE ORGANISATION

OF THE UNITED NATIONS

Economic and Social Council

The Economic and Social Council coordinates the work of the many UN Specialised Agencies. These carry out the economic and social role of the United Nations, trying to improve living standards in poorer parts of the world. The work of the Specialised Agencies is dealt with on pages 21–29.

The Secretariat

The UN Secretariat is like a civil service for all the other parts of the United Nations. It is headed by the Secretary General of the UN, currently Kofi Annan of Ghana. The job of Secretary General is a very important one as he is present at all major UN events and can act as a personal mediator in disputes between states.

The International Court of Justice

The International Court of Justice, based in The Hague, deals with human rights issues.

UN Mission of Observers in Prevalka (UNMOP)

Date Sent	Numbers Involved	Nations Involved
1993	27 military observers 3 foreign civilian staff	22 countries

Monitoring the demilitarisation of the Prevalka peninsula, a strategic area disputed by Croatia and the Federal Republic of Yugoslavia.

UN Mission in Bosnia-Herzegovina(UNMBH)

Date Sent	Numbers Involved	Nations Involved
1995	1,458 uniformed personnel 302 foreign civilian staff	43 countries (including UK)

Range of duties relating to law enforcement activities in Bosnia and Herzegovina; also coordinates other UN activities in the country to do with humanitarian relief and refugees, demining, human rights, elections and rehabilitation of infrastructure and economic reconstruction.

UN Interim Administration Mission in Kosovo (UNMIK)

Date Sent	Numbers Involved	Nations Involved
1999	4,519 armed international police 4,600 civilian posts	49 countries

UN Resolution 1244 called upon UNMIK to: perform basic government functions; promote the establishment of self-government in Kosovo; create a political process to determine Kosovo's future status; coordinate humanitarian and disaster relief for all international agencies; support the reconstruction of key infrastructure; maintain law and order; promote human rights; and assure the safe return of all refugees and displaced persons to their homes in Kosovo.

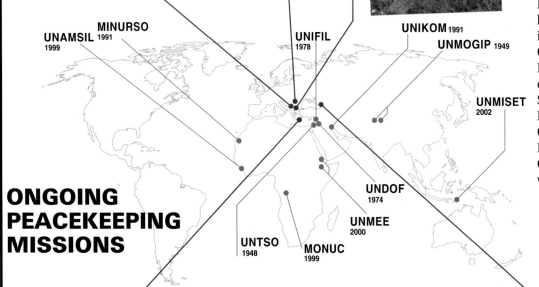

ONGOING PEACEKEEPING MISSIONS

UNAMSIL 1991
1999

MINURSO 1991

UNIFIL 1978

UNIKOM 1991

UNMOGIP 1949

UNMISET 2002

UNDOF 1974

UNMEE 2000

UNTSO 1948

MONUC 1999

In 2002 the UN had peacekeeping operations in Congo, Ethiopia, Eritrea, Sierra Leone, Western Sahara, East Timor, Kashmir, Bosnia, Cyprus, Georgia, Prevalka, Kosovo, Golan Heights, Kuwait and Lebanon.

UN Force in Cyprus (UNFICYP)

Date Sent	Numbers Involved	Nations Involved
1964	1,238 uniformed personnel 141 foreign civilian staff	9 countries (including UK)

Set up in 1964 to prevent further fighting between the Greek Cypriot and Turkish Cypriot communities. After the hostilities of 1974, responsibilities were expanded. UNFICYP remains on the island to supervise ceasefire lines, maintain the buffer zone and undertake humanitarian activities.

UN Observer Mission in Georgia (UNOMIG)

Date Sent	Numbers Involved	Nations Involved
1993	107 military observers 93 foreign civilian staff 176 local civilians	23 countries (including UK)

Established in 1993 to verify compliance with the ceasefire agreement between the government of Georgia and the Abkhaz authorities in Georgia. Mandate was expanded following the signing of the 1994 Ceasefire Agreement.

PEACEKEEPING AND THE UN

Forces drawn from UN members patrol a troubled area to try and keep the warring sides apart. These UN Forces are known as the 'Blue Berets' because of their distinctive uniform. Such a force has been used in the former Yugoslavia.

ACTIVITIES

1   What is the role of each of the following parts of the United Nations:

   a)   General Assembly?
   b)   Secretary General?
   c)   Security Council?
   d)   Economic and Social Council?
   e)   International Court of Justice?

2   Why is the UN more effective in its peacekeeping role than it used to be?

3   Write a 150 word newspaper report in which you summarise the UN's peacekeeping activities around the world. Mention the main areas where it is involved and the reasons for UN involvement.

4   *"The actions taken by the UN Security Council are useless."*

   Study the actions listed on page 66. Do you agree that they are useless? Give reasons for your answer.

The effectiveness of the UN has grown since the end of the Cold War. The United States and the Soviet Union used to block each other's attempts to find peace in international disputes, but now the UN is free from that type of political action.

When the Iraqis invaded Kuwait in 1990, the UN took collective security action to remove them. The American and British forces who fought in the Gulf did so under the banner of the United Nations and they were there as representatives of the whole UN organisation.

FACTFILE: UN action

The UN tries to prevent the outbreak of war by making countries co-operate with each other. If war does break out, the UN tries to bring it to an end as quickly as possible. The UN is also trying to limit the spread of weapons and reduce the numbers of particularly dangerous chemical and nuclear weapons in the world.

The UN Security Council has a number of options when dealing with a conflict.

Fact-Finding Missions
The UN can send a delegation to investigate a conflict and it will then report back to the General Assembly and the Security Council.

Military Observers
UN officials patrol a ceasefire arrangement between countries which are engaged in a conflict.

Economic Sanctions
The UN can ask member states to stop trading with a country if they want to put that nation under pressure. Economic sanctions were imposed on Serbia to try and change its policy in Bosnia.

Arms Sanctions
The UN can ask member states to stop dealing in arms and munitions with a particular country. This can be used to cut off supplies which are being used in a war.

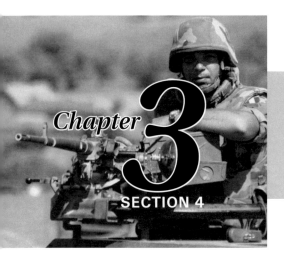

MILITARY ALLIANCES
THE ARMS RACE

What you will learn:

1 The development of nuclear weapons and the theory of deterrence.

2 Progress in arms reduction treaties.

From the early 1950s through to the late 1980s the USA and the USSR were engaged in an 'Arms Race'. Both sides tried to develop more and more nuclear weapons, and to make them ever more powerful and accurate. 'Weapons of Mass Destruction' is a term often used to describe modern weapons which are based on nuclear and chemical technology.

DETERRENCE
Both sides argued that having all these weapons made the world a safer place. The two superpowers disagreed with each other on many issues of ideology, but each was frightened to start a war with the other. They knew that whoever started the war could not win, because their opponents were so heavily armed. The outcome of nuclear war would have been destruction for both sides. Because they knew what the consequences would be, this became known as the Theory of Deterrence.

CHEMICAL AND BIOLOGICAL WEAPONS
During the Cold War both sides investigated the use of chemical and biological weapons. These were banned under international law but research into them was no secret. Chemical weapons can take various forms. Poisonous gases could be used directly against people. Chemical agents could be used to contaminate the water supply or to spread disease. It is known that Iraq used chemical weapons during the Gulf War and against the Kurdish people in the north of Iraq. In 2002 the Russian military special forces used a nerve gas against terrorists holding hostages in a Moscow theatre, killing the terrorists and many of their captives.

The mushroom cloud created by the explosion of an atomic bomb dropped on the Japanese city of Hiroshima on 6 August 1945. The American Super-Fortress aircraft which carried the bomb was called 'Enola Gay' after the mother of the pilot.

THE NUCLEAR AGE
The race to produce nuclear weapons began during World War II. It was known that it would be possible to develop weapons with vast destructive power and both the Americans and the Germans started programmes to produce 'the bomb'.

Time ran out for the German scientists with the defeat of their armies in May 1945, just at the time when the Americans had made the breakthrough. They continued the development work and in August 1945 two atomic bombs were dropped on the Japanese cities of Hiroshima and Nagasaki.

The destruction was enormous. Seventy thousand people died within seconds in Hiroshima, and over 250,000 died there in total. The figures were repeated at Nagasaki.

The bombs used on Japan in 1945 were tiny compared to the devices developed in the 1970s and '80s. These could have a destructive force 5,000 times as great as the Hiroshima bomb. The attack on Japan was carried out by dropping the bombs from aircraft. Nowadays it is possible to deliver the nuclear warhead to its target in many different ways: by land-based cruise missile, by submarine-launched missile, by shell, by bomb or by intercontinental rocket.

The prospect of nuclear war frightened the world from the 1960s until the late 1980s. The superpowers possessed the weapons to wipe out the earth's population many times over. Today there are still thousands of nuclear weapons in existence, but the chances of them being used have lessened. Leaders of both the USA and the USSR tried, at various times, to make agreements to reduce the number of nuclear and conventional weapons held by each side. (See the Factfile opposite.)

(See the Factfile opposite.)

ACTIVITIES

1 *"The destructive power of nuclear weapons is enormous."*

   Give evidence to support this statement.

2 How do modern nuclear weapons differ from those dropped on Japan in 1945?

3 What is meant by 'the Arms Race'?

4 What is meant by 'Deterrence'?

5 What major breakthrough in limiting nuclear weapons was achieved in 1987?

6 Why was the START 2 agreement delayed?

7 Study the information below then answer the question which follows.

   "The USA has always had more nuclear weapons than Russia."
   View of a defence journalist

   To what extent is the defence journalist guilty of making selective use of facts?

8 What conclusions can be reached about the success of Arms Limitation Treaties since the early 1970s?

FACTFILE: Arms Agreements

1963 Partial Test Ban Treaty
The USA, the USSR and the UK agreed to stop testing nuclear weapons in the atmosphere. France continued to do so.

1968 Nuclear Non-Proliferation Treaty
This treaty was designed to stop the spread of the knowledge and the technology required to make nuclear weapons. In theory each country with nuclear weapons must have developed them by itself, with its own expertise and raw materials.

1972 Strategic Arms Limitation Treaty (SALT 1)
This treaty set upper limits for how many long-range nuclear missiles each country could have.

1979 SALT 2
Extended the previous talks and set new limits for strategic nuclear missiles.

1987 INF Treaty (Intermediate Nuclear Forces)
This treaty dealt with short- and medium-range nuclear missiles—the type which could be used in Europe. All land based weapons in these categories were to be destroyed within three years, and the USA and USSR had access to each other's sites for verification of the Treaty. The INF Treaty did not include submarine launched missiles.

1990 Conventional Forces in Europe Treaty (CFE)
The Warsaw Pact countries always had a huge advantage in numbers of conventional weapons. This treaty evened out the military balance in Europe, setting maximum numbers for tanks, artillery, armoured vehicles etc.

1991 Strategic Arms Reduction Treaty (START 1)
Around 30% of the really destructive Intercontinental Ballistic Missiles were destroyed. These are the type of missiles which could be launched from the USA and wipe out Moscow within an hour. There was to be a maximum of 6,000 nuclear warheads by the year 2000, each still capable of killing hundreds of thousands of people.

1993 START 2
This treaty built on the progress made in START 1. All Intercontinental Ballistic Missiles were to be eliminated from the year 2003 on. Only submarine launched and mobile warheads were to remain. The total number of nuclear warheads was to be reduced from 6,000 to about 3,500.

START 1 came into force in 1994. START 2, although it was agreed in the early 1990s, was held up because Russia was seriously angered by the expansion of NATO into Eastern Europe, US threats to break the Antiballistic Missile (ABM) treaty and being ignored by NATO when the decision was made to bomb Serbia/Kosovo.

It was not until May 2002 that the USA and Russia reached a new agreement at a meeting between Presidents Putin and Bush in Moscow. The treaty aims to cut the nuclear arsenals of each side from the current levels of between six and seven thousand to around two thousand by 2012.

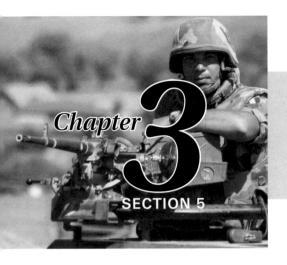

Chapter 3
SECTION 5

MILITARY ALLIANCES
THE WAR ON TERRORISM

What you will learn:

1 The reaction of the major powers to international terrorism.

2 The impact of their actions by 2003.

On 11 September 2001 an Al Qaeda cell hijacked four airliners at Boston. These were turned into 'flying bombs'. Two struck the World Trade Centre buildings in New York causing them to collapse. One was flown into the Pentagon building in Washington (the HQ of the American Armed Forces). The fourth plane crashed in countryside following a struggle between the hijackers and passengers—it is thought that its intended target was the White House.

The events of 11 September 2001 changed attitudes towards global security. For the first time since the Japanese attack on Pearl Harbour in 1941, including the whole Cold War period, the USA itself became a target. President Bush reacted by effectively 'declaring war' on terrorism. The perceived enemy was the Al Qaeda organisation led by Osama bin Laden.

Bin Laden was accused of having planned and carried out other terror attacks on American targets. These included detonat-

ing bombs to devastating effect at US embassies in East Africa and a suicide attack by a small boat on an American warship anchored in Yemen.

INTERNATIONAL RESPONSE
The USA was keen to involve other countries in the response to these attacks. Rather than making a unilateral response, the USA formed a coalition with other countries to make a multilateral response. The UK was one of the most active countries in its support for the 'coalition against terrorism'. This type of

President George Bush and Prime Minister Tony Blair led the demands for the world community to combat terrorism seriously after the destruction of the Twin Towers in New York.

coalition had been formed once before—in 1991 when a US-led coalition forced Iraq to withdraw after invading Kuwait in what was known as the Gulf War.

The immediate aims of the coalition were:

❧ to bring Osama bin Laden and other Al Qaeda leaders to justice;

❧ to prevent Osama bin Laden and the Al Qaeda network from posing a continuing terrorist threat;

❧ to ensure that Afghanistan ceased to harbour and support international terrorism and to destroy terrorist training camps in Afghanistan;

❧ to change the leadership of Afghanistan (i.e. remove the Taliban from power) to ensure that they would stop sponsoring terrorism.

The wider objectives of the coalition were:

❖ to do everything possible to eliminate the threat posed by international terrorism;

❖ to deter states from supporting or harbouring international terrorist groups;

❖ reintegration of Afghanistan as a responsible member of the international community and an end to its self-imposed isolation.

The objectives of the coalition were to be achieved by:

✳ isolating the Taliban regime from all international support;

✳ taking direct action against Osama bin Laden, the Al Qaeda network and the terrorist facilities in Afghanistan;

✳ taking political and military action to defeat the Taliban regime, including support-

ing the Pushtoon groups and the Northern Alliance in their opposition to the Taliban;

✳ providing economic and political support to Afghanistan's neighbours to help them with the costs of the conflict (they had been inundated with refugees);

✳ building the widest possible international coalition, with maximum UN support;

✳ taking immediate steps to deal with the humanitarian crisis confronting Afghanistan and to help neighbouring countries deal with the refugee problem.

HOW SUCCESSFUL WAS THE WAR ON TERRORISM?

In 2003 the war on terrorism was ongoing. The international coalition against terrorism received widespread support. Countries involved included the

With either the youngest or the oldest members of the family riding overladen donkeys, a group of Afghan refugees make their way through a narrow passage as they leave the nearest village to the front line, not far from the town of Khanabad, Kunduz Province, for fear of new fights in northern Afghanistan.

USA, Canada, the UK, France, Belgium, Germany, the Czech Republic, Romania, Russia, Japan, New Zealand, Jordan and Turkey.

Some countries, such as the UK, committed troops to the coalition. In other cases, for instance many of the Arab nations of the Middle East, support came in the form of permission to use their airspace and air bases to support the missions on the ground in Afghanistan.

As well as the direct action taken within Afghanistan many countries stepped up their own action against potential terrorist activity. Many suspects were arrested and the security services monitored the activities of others. Al Qaeda was thought to have many 'sleeper cells' around the world which could become active at any time.

In addressing its main aims, the coalition had limited success.

Taliban defeated
The Taliban regime in Afghanistan was defeated. Coalition forces supported the Northern Alliance in its campaign to overthrow the government. A new government was installed and steps were taken towards restoring democracy in Afghanistan. However, the population of the country is deeply divided and it was not an easy task to restore peace to society there.

Al Qaeda removed
Al Qaeda training camps were located and destroyed. Most had been abandoned as the Taliban and Al Qaeda were forced to retreat.

It is hard to say whether international support for Al Qaeda was stopped. Obviously, few governments could openly support Al Qaeda but their funding and backing were often received by the organisation through obscure and anonymous links. Countries like Iraq did continue to provide moral support to the Al Qaeda organisation.

Osama bin Laden
Osama bin Laden was thought to have escaped to Pakistan. The mountainous areas on the borders of Afghanistan and Pakistan are vast and inhospitable making it difficult for Coalition forces to search them.

Iraq
In the summer of 2002 the USA began to make plans for a military assault on Iraq aimed at bringing down the government of Saddam Hussein. While this may have been a popular move in the USA, other Coalition members were less enthusiastic about the possible consequences. The UN applied pressure to Iraq and late in 2002 was given permission to send Weapons Inspectors to Iraq. This move may have delayed military action but many observers felt that President Bush was still determined to launch an assault on Saddam Hussein's government. He did not just want to make sure that Iraq did not have weapons of mass destruction, he wanted 'regime change' to make sure that Iraq would never have the capability of developing them.

Attacks continue
Other examples of international terrorism deflected attention away from Afghanistan. Late in 2002 a series of bombs in the Indonesian tourist resort of Bali killed over 200 people, mainly Australians. Chechen terrorists took more than 700 hostages in a Moscow theatre and many were killed when Russian special forces tried to free them.

These incidents may or may not have been directly linked to Al Qaeda. However, the organisation of Al Qaeda is loose and unstructured with cells within it that are almost totally independent of each other. This is partly why it is such a difficult enemy to confront.

THREATS TO WORLD PEACE
Early in 2003 the global security situation was more fragile than at any time for many years. The USA was poised to launch an attack on Iraq depending on the outcome of investigations by United Nations weapons inspectors. The UK looked likely to support President Bush in such an attack, although other major European countries, including France and Germany, did not give their support. North Korea, one of the few Communist countries left in the world, was restarting its nuclear arms programme after being named as part of an 'axis of evil' by President Bush. North Korea had been in deadlock with South Korea since the end of the Korean War in 1953. This was the last part of the Cold War that was still ongoing.

ACTIVITIES

1 Describe briefly the events of 11 September 2001.

2 What is a 'coalition'?

3 What were the aims of the coalition against terrorism?

4 *"The international coalition did not have widespread support."*

   Why could the person making this statement be accused of exaggeration?

5 How successful was the coalition in meeting its main aims?

6 Describe terrorist activities since 11 September 2001.

Chapter 4

LIVING IN EUROPE

What you will learn:

1 The differences in lifestyles across Europe.

LIVING AND WORKING IN EUROPE

Most people born in Scotland think of themselves as Scottish or British. However, increasingly it is our 'European' identity that is important. Many of the rules and laws which govern our lives are now applied Europe-wide. We have rights and responsibilities which apply to us because of our European citizenship.

All EU citizens have the right to live and work in any other EU country. This freedom of movement is seen as an important part of the creation of a 'united Europe'. There are no physical barriers to movement. Education and professional qualifications from one EU member state should be recognised in all others. People also have rights of access to social services and health care in other EU countries.

Internal borders and passport controls have largely been scrapped. People can travel from Portugal to Denmark, passing through Spain, France, Luxembourg, Belgium, Holland and Germany without being stopped at borders. The United Kingdom chose to retain passport checks at airports and seaports but is now out of step with the rest of Europe.

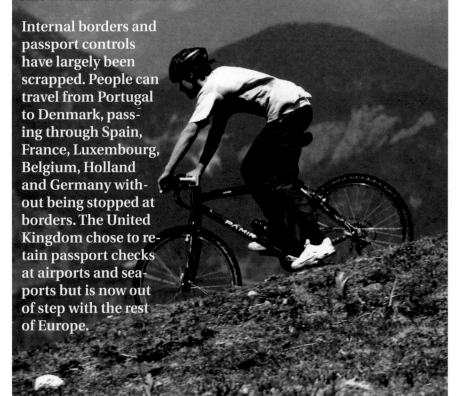

Border checks on entering the EU from outside are very different. The EU is an attractive place for asylum seekers and refugees from around the world, but particularly from Eastern Europe and the former Soviet Union. Citizens of countries outwith the EU do not have an automatic right to enter and settle in EU countries.

Many schools in Scotland have close links with Europe. Schools may have 'partner schools' through schemes such as the EU's COMENIUS project. Schools may also operate exchanges with schools in Europe or run trips and visits to other European countries.

ACTIVITIES

1 Do you consider yourself to be Scottish, British or European? Explain your answer.

2 What rights do Scottish people have in relation to living and working in Europe?

3 Find out what European links exist in your own school.

	EU Average	Germany	Spain	France	Italy	Netherlands	UK
Population (Million)		82.8	39.4	59.3	57.6	15.9	59.5
Unemployment (2000) (%)	8.2	7.9	14.1	9.5	10.5	3.0	5.5
Families below poverty line (%)	26	24	25	28	23	21	33
Spending on social services as proportion of GDP	27.6	29.6	20.0	30.3	25.3	28.1	26.9
Employment Rate for women (%)	54.0	57.1	40.3	55.1	39.6	63.6	64.8
Life Expectancy (Male)	74.6	74.3	75.3	74.9	75.8	75.2	74.3
Life Expectancy (Female)	80.9	80.7	82.5	82.3	82.4	80.5	80.7
People over 65 as a percentage of those aged 15–64	24	24	25	24	27	20	24
25-year-olds who have completed upper secondary school (%)	76	84	61	79	63	76	90

Table 4.1

Table 4.1 gives comparative information on living standards within the major EU member states.

ACTIVITIES

MAKING CONCLUSIONS

Modern Studies questions at both Intermediate and Standard Grade often ask students to make conclusions based on information they have been given. A simple conclusion deals with only one variable or factor at a time. Complex conclusions deal with the relationship between two or more factors. The Activities below are divided into simple and complex conclusions.

Simple Conclusions

1 Which country has the best:
(NB - remember that 'best' does not always mean the highest figure)
   a) unemployment rate?
   b) record for families living below the poverty line?
   c) record for spending on social services?
   d) life expectancy for men?
   e) life expectancy for women?
   f) record for people staying on at school?

2 Which country has the poorest:
   a) unemployment rate?
   b) record for families living below the poverty line?
   c) record for spending on social services?
   d) life expectancy for men?
   e) life expectancy for women?
   f) record for people staying on at school?

Complex Conclusions

3 What link can you see between unemployment and the percentage of people staying on at school?

4 *"Living standards in the UK are good compared to the rest of the EU."*

Give reasons to support and reasons to oppose this view.

Overall do you agree with this view?

GDP per head

PURCHASING POWER

€000

EU Average	16.6	
Belgium	18.8	
Denmark	19.1	
Germany	18.3	
Greece	10.5	
Spain	12.6	
France	17.8	
Ireland	14.1	
Luxembourg	26.9	
Netherlands	17.3	
Austria	18.8	
Portugal	11.4	
Finland	15.1	
Sweden	16.2	
UK	16.4	

Figure 4.1

Figure 4.1 shows GDP per head in terms of purchasing power.

STANDARD OF LIVING

Ownership of Certain Items per 1000 people (late 1990s)

	Telephones	Private Cars	Television Sets
Belgium	436	416	450
Denmark	590	309	530
Germany	456	488	560
Greece	458	177	350
Spain	365	344	400
France	537	430	580
Ireland	428	242	300
Italy	423	518	430
Luxembourg	543	567	350
Netherlands	500	383	540
Austria	449	433	500
Portugal	330	357	300
Finland	545	368	630
Sweden	679	409	670
UK	470	373	430
EU Average	461	422	489
USA	563	N A	816
Japan	467	N A	619

Table 4.2

ACTIVITIES

1 *"Countries in North-west Europe have higher GDP than countries in Southern Europe."*

Give evidence to support this viewpoint.

2 What conclusions can be made about ownership of telephones, private cars and television sets in different countries?

EDUCATION

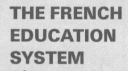

THE GERMAN EDUCATION SYSTEM

Germany is a federal country. This means that each region (Land) has considerable independence. The organisation of the education system varies significantly from region to region. Pre-school education takes place in Kindergarten up to the age of 6. From age 6 to age 10 pupils attend a Primary School or Grundschule. The transition period between primary and secondary education is known as the Orienterungsstufe. This lasts from age 10 to age 12. Pupils are then divided into different schools depending on the type of course they are suited to. Gymnasium is the most academic school; the other types are Realschule, Hauptschule and Gesamtschule.

The length of the school day and the school week vary from region to region. In most areas pupils start school around 8 a.m. and work until about 1.30 p.m. In some areas schools are open on Saturday mornings.

At age 16 pupils can receive a lower secondary leaving certificate. Some choose to stay on at school and enter the Gymnasium Oberstufe or the Berufsfachschulen (Vocational School). Those Gymnasium pupils wanting to go to university must sit the Abiturprufung.

THE FRENCH EDUCATION SYSTEM

Education in France is administered from Paris by the Ministry of Education. Individual schools do have considerable flexibility to decide the nature of the subjects they offer. Most choose to specialise in particular areas.

Pre-school education for those aged 2–6 is optional but most children from 3 upwards attend an école maternelle. From age 6 to age 11 children attend école élémentaire, and from age 11 to age 15 they go to a collège (lower secondary school). At age 15 they progress to one of the different types of lycée. Lycée d'enseignement général et technologique, or LEGT, (general and technical upper secondary) and lycée professionnel, or LP, (vocational upper secondary) are the two main types.

The school year is made up of 180 days between September and June. Schools are open six days a week but there are no classes on Wednesday and Saturday afternoons.

At the end of their collège education pupils are awarded a brevet (national certificate). Pupils who go on to attend the LEGT are entered for the baccalauréat. Those who go to the LP are entered for the certificat d'aptitude professionnel.

HOUSING

Since the 1980s home ownership has become the norm in the UK. Prior to then many people rented their homes, either from local authorities or from private landlords. The Conservative governments of the 1980s made the extension of home ownership one of their policy priorities.

Home ownership is not so common in most other EU countries. This means that people have less of their wealth 'tied up' in property. They can spend more of their money as they earn it and as a result may enjoy a better standard of living. The concept of suburban housing schemes with many detached, semi-detached and terraced houses with their own gardens is typical in the UK. Similar housing developments are relatively rare in Europe where most housing is in the form of flats and apartments. Detached houses are usually individually designed and built.

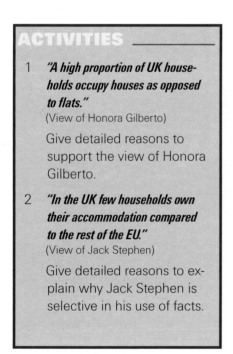

ACTIVITIES

1   *"A high proportion of UK households occupy houses as opposed to flats."*
    (View of Honora Gilberto)

    Give detailed reasons to support the view of Honora Gilberto.

2   *"In the UK few households own their accommodation compared to the rest of the EU."*
    (View of Jack Stephen)

    Give detailed reasons to explain why Jack Stephen is selective in his use of facts.

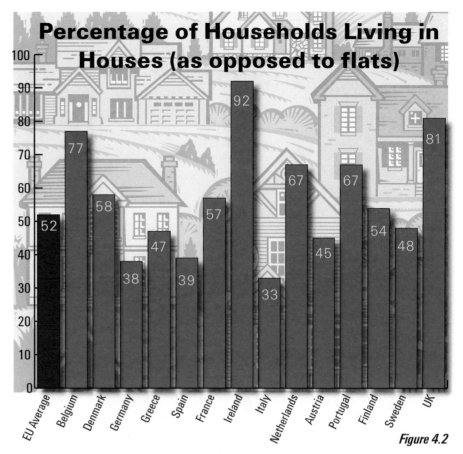

Figure 4.2

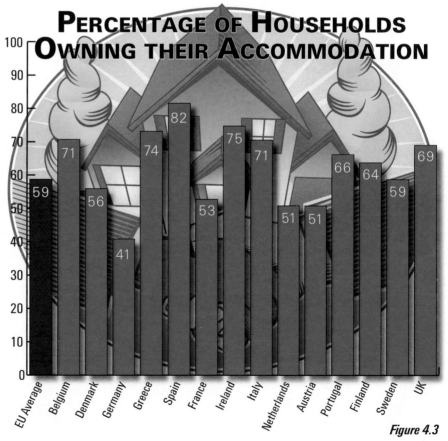

Figure 4.3

GERMANY

Population 82,797,408

Age structure	%	Male	Female
0–14 years	16	6,679,930	6,333,110
15–64 years	68	28,638,814	27,693,630
65 years and over	16	5,133,121	8,318,803

Ethnic Groups

German	91.5%
Turkish	2.4%
Other	6.1%

Religions

Protestant	38%
Roman Catholic	34%
Muslim	1.7%
Unaffiliated or other	26.3%

Net migration rate
4.01 migrant(s)/ 1,000 population

Population growth rate 0.29%

Birth rate 9.35 births/1,000 population

Death rate 10.49 deaths/1,000 population

INFANT MORTALITY RATE
4.77 deaths/1,000 live births

TOTAL FERTILITY RATE
1.38 children born/woman

LIFE EXPECTANCY AT BIRTH
Total population 77.44 years
Male 74.3 years
Female 80.75 years

Sex ratio at birth	1.06 male/female
under 15 years	1.05 male/female
15–64 years	1.03 male/female
65 years and over	0.62 male/female
total population	0.96 male/female

Languages: German

ITALY

Population 57,634,327

Age structure	%	Male	Female
0–14 years	14%	4,220,973	3,977,962
15–64 years	68%	19,413,219	19,596,668
65 years and over	18%	4,297,962	6,127,543

Ethnic Groups

Italian (includes small clusters of German-, French-, and Slovene-Italians in the north and Albanian-Italians and Greek-Italians in the south)

Religions

Predominantly Roman Catholic with mature Protestant and Jewish communities and a growing Muslim immigrant community.

Net migration rate
1.74 migrant(s)/ 1,000 population

Population growth rate 0.09%

Birth rate 9.13 births/1,000 population

Death rate 9.99 deaths/1,000 population

INFANT MORTALITY RATE
5.92 deaths/1,000 live births

TOTAL FERTILITY RATE
1.18 children born/woman

LIFE EXPECTANCY AT BIRTH
Total population 79.03 years
Male 75.85 years
Female 82.41 years

Sex ratio at birth	1.06 male/female
under 15 years	1.06 male/female
15–64 years	0.99 male/female
65 years and over	0.70 male/female
total population	0.94 male/female

Languages: Italian, German (parts of the Trentino-Alto Adige region are predominantly German-speaking), French (small French-speaking minority in Valle d'Aosta region), Slovene (Slovene-speaking minority in the Trieste-Gorizia area)

UNITED KINGDOM

Population **59,511,464**

Age structure	%	Male	Female
0–14 years	19	5,816,313	5,519,479
15–64 years	65	19,622,152	19,228,938
65 years and over	16	3,864,612	5,459,970

Ethnic Groups

English	81.5%
Scottish	9.6%
Irish	2.4%
Welsh	1.9%
Ulster	1.8%
West Indian, Indian, Pakistani, and other	2.8%

Religions

Anglican	27 million
Roman Catholic	9 million
Muslim	1 million
Presbyterian	800,000
Methodist	760,000
Sikh	400,000
Hindu	350,000
Jewish	300,000

Net migration rate 1.07 migrant(s)/ 1,000 population

Population growth rate 0.25%

Birth rate 11.76 births/1,000 population

Death rate 10.38 deaths/1,000 population

INFANT MORTALITY RATE 5.63 deaths/1,000 live births

TOTAL FERTILITY RATE 1.74 children born/woman

LIFE EXPECTANCY AT BIRTH

Total population	77.66 years
Male	74.97 years
Female	80.49 years

Sex ratio at birth	1.05 male/female
under 15 years	1.05 male/female
15-64 years	1.02 male/female
65 years and over	0.71 male/female
total population	0.97 male/female

Languages: English, Welsh (about 26% of the population of Wales), Scottish form of Gaelic (about 60,000 in Scotland)

FRANCE

Population **59,329,691**

Age structure	%	Male	Female
0–14 years	19%	5,719,502	5,448,608
15–64 years	65%	19,345,269	19,322,902
65 years and over	16%	3,849,783	5,643,627

Ethnic Groups

Celtic and Latin with Teutonic, Slavic, North African, Indo-chinese and Basque minorities

Religions

Roman Catholic	90%
Protestant	2%
Muslim	1%
Jewish	1%
Unaffiliated	6%

Net migration rate 0.66 migrant(s)/ 1,000 population

Population growth rate 0.38%

Birth rate 12.27 births/1,000 population

Death rate 9.14 deaths/1,000 population

INFANT MORTALITY RATE 4.51 deaths/1,000 live births

TOTAL FERTILITY RATE 1.75 children born/woman

LIFE EXPECTANCY AT BIRTH

Total population	74.85 years
Male	74.85 years
Female	82.89 years

Sex ratio at birth	1.05 male/female
under 15 years	1.05 male/female
15-64 years	1.00 male/female
65 years and over	0.68 male/female
total population	0.95 male/female

Languages: French 100%, rapidly declining regional dialects and languages (Provençal, Breton, Alsatian, Corsican, Catalan, Basque, Flemish)

FAMILY LIFE

	EU Average	France	Germany	Italy	Spain	UK
Average Household Size	2.4	2.35	2.15	2.65	3.2	2.25
Proportion of one-person households	28	30	35	23	12	29
Proportion of people living in household with 2 adults and 3 or more children	7	9	4	5	4	8
Divorce Rate (per 1000 people per year)	1.8	2.0	2.1	0.5	0.8	2.9
Percentage of births outwith marriage	23	37	16	8	11	34
Percentage of children living with one parent	9	9	9	6	5	16

Table 4.3

LEISURE ACTIVITIES

In most other European countries eating out in restaurants and cafes is more common than in the UK. Although people in countries such as France and Germany consume, on average, more alcohol than those in the UK, drunken behaviour is very unusual. People drink in a more sociable way and 'binge' drinking is less common.

The family plays a bigger role in leisure time for many Europeans. For example, in Germany families are more likely to take part in activities as a group. In the UK it is now more common for different family members to take part in their own leisure activities with their friends.

Number of Registered Football Players Per 1000 People in Selected EU Countries

Country	Population (million)	Number of Players	Percentage of population registered as footballers
Austria	8.1	253,576	3.1%
Belgium	10.2	390,468	3.8%
England	50	2,550,000	5.1%
Germany	82.2	5,260,320	6.4%
Netherlands	15.9	962,397	6.1%
Ireland	3.6	124,615	3.5%
Italy	57.8	1,420,160	2.5%
Spain	39.4	408,135	1.1%
Scotland	5	135,474	2.7%
France	59.5	1,692,205	2.8%

Table 4.4

ACTIVITIES

1. Study the information about the UK and the three other European countries on pages 78 and 79. Write a report in which you compare the people of these countries under the following headings:

   ✎ Population
   ✎ Age Structure
   ✎ Changes in Population
   ✎ Sex Ratio
   ✎ Life Expectancy
   ✎ Ethnic Groups
   ✎ Language

2. What conclusions can be reached about family life in the UK compared to family life in the other EU countries listed in Table 4.5?

3. *"It is no surprise that Scotland and England do badly in world football – they have a small proportion of registered players."*

   Statement by journalist

   To what extent could the journalist be accused of being selective in her/his use of facts?

Stereotypes
A Word of Caution

Stereotypes are 'caricature'-type images of people. Europeans have a stereotype image of 'the typical Scotsman'. Scottish people know that the stereotype image is not an accurate depiction of most Scottish people. Stereotypes have a hint of truth about them but they exaggerate preconceptions and myths about national identities.

Modern Studies aims to promote informed attitudes in students. You should not use stereotypes to describe people from other European countries. These can be upsetting and offensive to people.